Here is what the critics are saying about *The Best of St. Thomas and St. John, U.S. Virgin Islands* and Pamela Acheson's writing:

"Visitors seeking advice on warmer climes can find it in *The Best of St. Thomas and St. John, U.S. Virgin Islands* by Pamela Acheson." —*Publisher's Weekly*

"A near-guarantee of a great trip." —*Independent Publisher*

"Pamela Acheson shares her intimate knowledge of hotels, inns, bars, restaurants, shops and attractions." —*Virgin Islands Weekly Journal*

"Essential to getting the most out of any trip." —*Midwest Book Review*

"A lighthearted guidebook...full of insider tips and recommendations." —*Essentially America*

"The absolute best guidebook on St. Thomas and St. John." —*Peter Island Morning Sun*

"A valid and nifty guide to wonderful places." —*The Naples Daily News*

"Travelers to St. Thomas want to invest in *The Best of St. Thomas and St. John, U.S. Virgin Islands.*" —*Orlando Sentinel*

Pamela Acheson is one "of our extraordinary writers." —*Fodor's Caribbean*

"I want to be there, wanna go back down
and lie beside the sea there
with a tin cup for a chalice
fill it up with red wine
and I'm chewin' on a honeysuckle vine."

—*Jimmy Buffett*

THE BEST
OF
ST. THOMAS AND ST. JOHN,
U.S. VIRGIN ISLANDS

PAMELA ACHESON

TWO THOUSAND THREE ASSOCIATES
TTTA

Published by
TWO THOUSAND THREE ASSOCIATES
4180 Saxon Drive, New Smyrna Beach, Florida 32169
Voice: 1.800.598.5256 or 386.427.7876; Fax 386.423.7523

Library of Congress Cataloging-in-Publication Data
Acheson, Pamela.
    The best of St. Thomas and St. John, U.S. Virgin Islands / Pamela Acheson .
    p.   cm.
    Includes index.
    ISBN 0-9639905-1-9
    1. Saint Thomas (V.I.)--Guidebooks. 2. Saint John (V.I.)-
-Guidebooks   I. Title
    F2105.A64   1998
    917.297'22--dc21   98-48750
                                                    CIP

Printed in the United States of America

Fifth Printing April 2002

Photo Credits
Front Cover: Courtesy of U.S. Virgin Islands Division of Tourism
Back cover: Pamela Acheson

ISBN 0-9639905-1-9

10 9 8 7 6 5

for Aunt Jane
and
in memory of
my father

ACKNOWLEDGEMENTS
Special thanks to Martin Public Relations.

DISCLAIMER
The author has made every effort to ensure accuracy in this book but bear in mind that, despite what you hear about "island time," everything to do with vacationing in the Caribbean—schedules, restaurants, hotels, events, modes of transportation, etc.—can open, relocate, or close with remarkable speed. Neither the author nor the publisher are responsible for anyone's traveling or vacation experiences.

INTRODUCTION

Altogether there are about 60 islands, islets, and cays in the U.S. Virgin Islands. Most are uninhabited. The four main U.S. Virgin Islands are St. Thomas, little Water Island (just off the south shore of St. Thomas), St. John (two miles east of St. Thomas), and St. Croix, 40 miles to the south.

I love St. Thomas and St. John. Like brothers or sisters, they share similarities and differences. They complement each other, and they stand on their own. Despite their geographical similarities and the fact that they are only two miles apart, in many ways they are two entirely different destinations. Together they offer a mixed U.S. and Caribbean experience.

Although you'll find familiar U. S. staples like traffic jams and big macs and large resorts and uniformed park rangers, they're all entwined in an authentic Caribbean setting. You'll also find acres and acres of untouched land, intimate inns, tiny beachfront restaurants, a laid-back style of living, and absolutely spectacular scenery—tropical blue water lapping against classic crescents of white sand, steep green hills, beaches that will steal your heart. It's an "island experience" that is truly unique.

St. John and St. Thomas are U.S. Territories. The language is English (with the delightful island lilt). The currency is U.S. dollars. The flights are frequent. The weather, near perfect.

The two islands are only a twenty-minute ferry ride apart and on any day, on either or both of the islands, you can swim or snorkel in the crystal clear Caribbean, enjoy mountaintop views, some amazing jeep rides or hikes, a world-class dinner, and the glimmering lights on the water, over the water, and even under it.

There is truly something for everyone on these islands and it is my hope that *The Best of St. Thomas and St. John, U.S. Virgin Islands* will help anyone visiting these islands have a more hassle-free, enjoyable, and memorable Virgin Island vacation. So set your mind to island time and enjoy the adventure.

—P.A.

TABLE OF CONTENTS

SPECIAL FEATURES

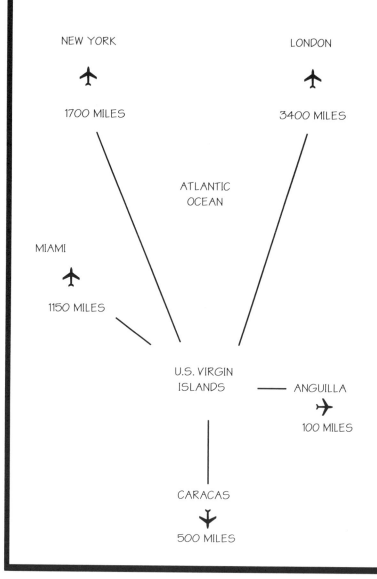

SECTION I

ST. THOMAS

RESORTS AND INNS
RESTAURANTS
BARS
SHOPPING
LUNCH BREAKS
BEACHES
WATERSPORTS
LANDSPORTS
ISLAND ATTRACTIONS

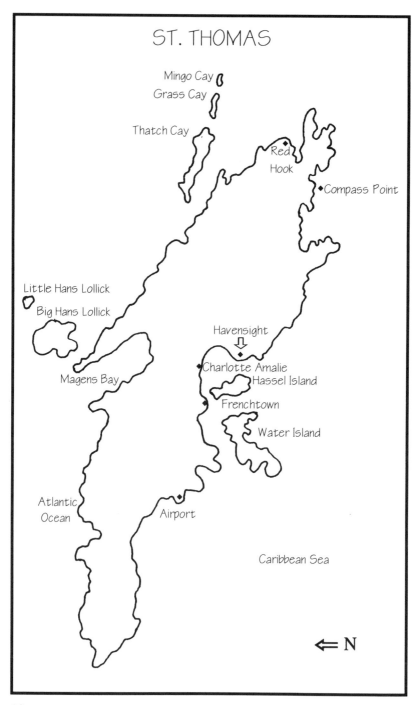

ST. THOMAS

Mingo Cay
Grass Cay
Thatch Cay
Red Hook
◆Compass Point
Little Hans Lollick
Big Hans Lollick
Havensight
◆Charlotte Amalie
Hassel Island
Magens Bay
Frenchtown
Water Island
Atlantic Ocean
Airport
Caribbean Sea
⇐ N

ABOUT ST. THOMAS

St. Thomas is a hugely popular destination and decidedly cosmopolitan. It's an island of world-class shopping, fine dining, and full-service resorts but it also has its share of traffic jams, honking horns, and cruise ship crowds. The overall atmosphere is lively and active. Restaurants are full and open late, beaches are busy with volleyball games, taxis are packed with people going somewhere, downtown streets are bustling with shoppers, and groups of snorkelers are checking out the underwater sights. On the other hand, you can easily find a quiet bar or an intimate table for two or a peaceful spot at the end of a beach.

St. Thomas is easy to reach (there's an international airport) and it's an easy place to be. The island offers all the comforts of home, yet it has a true Caribbean soul. It's a great place to go when you want to get away fast to tropical weather, when you want to spend your days at the beach and your nights out and about, when you want to really relax and do nothing, and when you want to be somewhere that is truly Caribbean and somewhat exotic but not totally unfamiliar.

St. Thomas, at 32 square miles, is the largest and most populated U.S. Virgin Island and about 50,000 people live there (whereas only 5,000 people live on the island of St. John, which is two miles to the east). St. Thomas is 13 miles long and its width varies from one to four miles, but this narrowness is deceiving since you almost always have to go up over a steep hill to get to the other side. The island is lushly tropical, rugged, and mountainous and ringed with crescents of white sand. Views from the hills are spectacular.

Most resorts are on the east end of St. Thomas, near Red Hook. Others are near Charlotte Amalie (it's pronounced ah-MAL-yuh). Most restaurants are in Charlotte Amalie, in Frenchtown (which is next to Charlotte Amalie), and out on the east end of the island. Some people think Charlotte Amalie is only for duty-free shoppers, but it also has many one-of-a-kind little shops and even people who hate to shop get smitten. It's also a lovely town. Look for stonework and brick walls, ornate gates and balconies, graceful archways, and colorful doors.

GREAT
ST. THOMAS SIGHTS

The sun rising on the beach

The clouds you can almost touch

The pelicans diving for their dinner

The amazing blues of the water

The lights of Charlotte Amalie

The cruise ships heading out in tandem
at the end of the day

The moon rising over the St. Thomas hills

The incredible colors of the sky
when the sun is setting

The seaplane taking off from the harbor

CHAPTER 1

GREAT
ST. THOMAS
RESORTS
&
INNS

"There is nothing which has yet been
contrived by man by which so much
happiness is produced as by
a good tavern or inn."
                              —*Samuel Johnson*

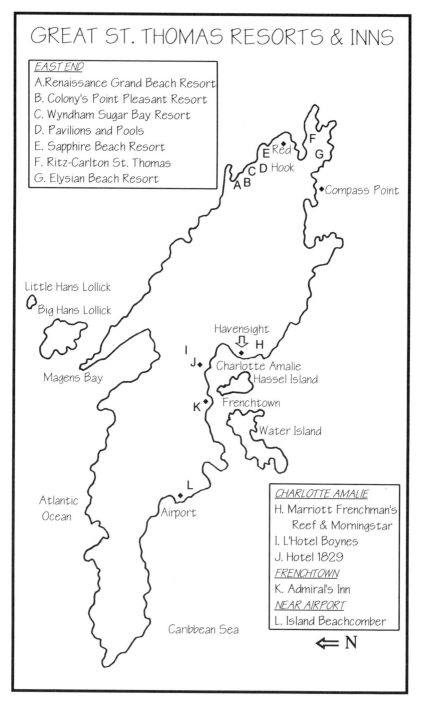

GREAT ST. THOMAS RESORTS & INNS

EAST END
A. Renaissance Grand Beach Resort
B. Colony's Point Pleasant Resort
C. Wyndham Sugar Bay Resort
D. Pavilions and Pools
E. Sapphire Beach Resort
F. Ritz-Carlton St. Thomas
G. Elysian Beach Resort

E Red F
C D Hook G
A B
◆Compass Point

Little Hans Lollick
Big Hans Lollick

Havensight
⇩ H
I
J◆
Charlotte Amalie
Magens Bay
Hassel Island
K◆
Frenchtown
Water Island

L
Atlantic
Ocean
Airport

Caribbean Sea

CHARLOTTE AMALIE
H. Marriott Frenchman's
   Reef & Morningstar
I. L'Hotel Boynes
J. Hotel 1829
FRENCHTOWN
K. Admiral's Inn
NEAR AIRPORT
L. Island Beachcomber

⇐ N

GREAT ST. THOMAS RESORTS & INNS

There are all kinds of great places to stay on St. Thomas: full-service resorts that you really never have to leave, intimate inns, motel-style beachfront hotels, condo-style units with full kitchens, and a wide range of rental villas.

Where you decide to stay on St. Thomas will depend a lot on what you want to do. Do you want to roll out of bed onto the beach, or spend the days visiting different beaches or exploring the island? Do you want to avoid shopping, or shop every day, or maybe just once? Do you want a big, full-service hotel with several restaurants right on the property or do you want a little inn? Or do you want the privacy of a villa?

Generally speaking, places to stay are either near Charlotte Amalie or about 25 minutes away, along the eastern end of the island. There are advantages to both locations. If you are near Charlotte Amalie, you are close to world-class shopping, many excellent restaurants and tourist attractions, and not that far from famous Magen's Bay Beach.

If you choose to stay on the east end of St. Thomas, you are more "out in the country." You are not far from a different set of restaurants and close to the little town of Red Hook, which has limited but interesting shopping. Red Hook is where ferries leave frequently for St. John and the British Virgin Islands (less frequent service is also available from downtown Charlotte Amalie). You are also close to the departure point for many charter boat day trips and you are near a number of very good beaches. At the east end resorts, you will also have stunning views of St. John and the British Virgin Islands in the distance.

Rental villas are scattered all over the island and can be found on the beach and high in the hills. Many overlook beautiful Magen's Bay.

This chapter first describes places to stay near or in Charlotte Amalie, followed by places along the east end of St. Thomas. Rates given are for two people without meals, and the range is from the lowest off-season rate to the highest on-season rate. Expect to pay an 8% tax.

17

ADMIRAL'S INN

This is a wonderful place to stay if you want a casual retreat and don't mind not being on a beach. It's set on a point with great views of the ocean, the harbor, and Charlotte Amalie. There's a nice pool and a good continental breakfast and you can easily walk to all the Frenchtown restaurants and on into town. The owners are exceptionally fine and helpful hosts.

Anne and Hal Borns bought this informal inn in 1992 and have been improving it ever since. It's built into the side of a steep little hill. There are 12 rooms in three wooden buildings that are painted in bright pinks, purples, blues, and yellows and have bright red tin roofs. (This was a 16-room inn until September of 1995 when Hurricane Marilyn blew away the entire second floor of an eight-unit building. Those two tall poles with flags flying from them used to be the outside corners of the second floor.)

Rooms are light and airy, a comfortable size, and modestly furnished in light oak or rattan. The four ocean-view rooms are the highest and have private balconies with a terrific view of nearby Water Island and the Caribbean Sea. You'll catch a glimpse of an occasional cruise ship crossing in the distance. These rooms each have a king size bed. The eight harbor view rooms are in two buildings that look out over St. Thomas harbor which, with the sparkling of the downtown lights, is a particularly pretty nighttime view. These rooms have one or two queen beds and terraces. There is also an efficiency apartment with a small kitchen. All rooms have air-conditioning, ceiling fans, and TVs. The extra pillows are an excellent touch. Every morning coffee and juices and a tempting assortment of tasty homemade breads and muffins are laid out near the pool. (Don't try to choose—just give in and have one of each!)

A large pool surrounded by a comfortable sunning deck is set half-way up the hill. The Admiral's Inn location is exceptionally convenient. It backs up to the popular Chart House restaurant, excellent Frenchtown restaurants and bars are virtually "next door," and Charlotte Amalie is a long walk or a two-minute cab ride. The airport is an easy ten minutes away. The inn is also within walking distance of the ferries to the British Virgin Islands. Car rentals are nearby and they will pick you up. Check for special diving, sailing, and honeymoon packages.

Pool, breakfast included in the room rate. 13 units. Villa Olga, Frenchtown, 00802. Res: 800-544-0493. Tel: 340-774-1376. Fax: 340-774-8010. http:// admirals.com/admiralsinn/. $89-$159.

18

HOTEL 1829

People often stay in this sophisticated historic inn because there's an excellent dinner restaurant and a wonderful bar on the first floor, because shopping and other restaurants are within easy walking distance, and because it has the warmth and friendliness you hope to find in a small establishment. Although there are only 15 rooms, the accommodations vary tremendously and range from luxurious to slightly spare.

The Hotel 1829 is located right on the eastern edge of downtown Charlotte Amalie, overlooking a park on Government Hill. A wide, steep set of stairs leads up to the original stone and stucco building, which was built by a French sea captain for his bride in 1829 and is now a National Historic Site. It's been a hotel since 1907. Graceful wrought iron gates lead into the tiny reception area and into the comfortable bar and restaurant.

The 15 units vary tremendously in size, furnishings, and price and there really is something for everyone here. The fanciest accommodations are quite beautiful. They are in the original building and are high-ceilinged suites with wooden beams, handsome stonework walls, upscale rattan furnishings, generous-size balconies, and views of the harbor.

The other suites and rooms are in a kind of compact sprawl that heads up a hill behind the original building and are reached by a narrow maze of outdoor stairways and walkways that crisscross charming tiny courtyards. These units are at various levels and are adequately but plainly furnished. Some look out at the small pool, others look out over the harbor, and some don't really look anywhere. A few rooms are extremely small.

All rooms have air-conditioning and cable television and many have private balconies. There is a small and very private pool surrounded by a little courtyard, a terrace garden with a superb harbor view that is open on-season for cocktails, and a Danish museum.

A serve-yourself continental breakfast with juices, breads, and cold cereals is set up in the bar each morning and you can eat inside or outside on the balcony. Downtown and the waterfront are just a few steps away.

Restaurant, bar, pool, gift shop, museum. 14 units. Government Hill, P.O. Box 1567, Charlotte Amalie, 00804. Res: 800-524-2002. Tel: 340-776-1829. Fax: 340-776-4313. $85-$245.

ISLAND BEACHCOMBER

This is a casual resort almost across from the airport. It's informal, fun, and on a nice beach. This is a place where you can live in your bathing suit and bare feet and slip on a cover-up for meals—even dinner.

The airport is across the street but there aren't that many large planes that fly to St. Thomas so noise isn't a continual problem. The 47 air-conditioned rooms are in several two-story buildings. Some are beachfront. Others look out on tropical gardens. All are just a few steps from the beach. Rooms are comfortable and decorated in pastels. All have balconies or terraces, small refrigerators, and televisions.

The watersports center offers scuba diving, waterskiing, and deep-sea fishing. The beach is long and calm. Guests gather day and night at the casual beach bar and the beachfront restaurant serves breakfast, lunch, and dinner. It's a ten-minute ride to many excellent restaurants and Charlotte Amalie.

Restaurant, bar, pool, beach, shop. 47 units. Lindbergh Bay, P.O. Box 302579, Charlotte Amalie, 00803. Res: 800-982-9898. Tel: 340-774-5250. Fax: 340-774-5615. www.st-thomas.com/islandbeachcomber. $100-$145.

L'HOTEL BOYNES

Set into a hillside with stunning views of Charlotte Amalie and the harbor, this conveniently-located bed and breakfast is a comfortable retreat within walking distance of many restaurants and shops.

A wrought iron gate, painted glistening white, leads to this 18th-century stone and brick building that is listed on the National Register of Historic Homes and is now an inviting bed and breakfast. Inside you'll find 12' high ceilings, teak floors, stone walls, mahogany doors, and antique furniture (check out the pump organ in the lobby). Each room is individually decorated with style and named. In "The Whimsy," which was once part of a kitchen, a huge old stone Dutch oven frames the head of the bed. Another has its own private balcony. All rooms have TV/VCRs and are air-conditioned. A long balcony with a decorative, wrought iron railing is a great place to catch a stunning view of the harbor and there's a cozy pool for a cool dip.

Pool; breakfast and transportation to the beach included in the room rate. 8 units. P.O. 11611, Charlotte Amalie, 00802. Res: 800-377-2905. Tel: 340-774-5511. Fax: 340-774-8509. www.hotelboynes.vi. $105-$195.

20

MARRIOTTS FRENCHMAN'S REEF & MORNING STAR

Sparkling from an extraordinary $52-million renovation, these two sister resorts, Frenchman's Reef and Morning Star, are at the opposite ends of the same property and share the same facilities. Together they form one giant, remarkably complete, full-service resort that you just never, ever have to leave.

Frenchman's Reef and Morning Star are two completely different places to stay. Frenchman's Reef is a huge, eight-story hotel, along with several two-story wings, perched dramatically on a cliff. The duty-free shops, fitness center, swimming pools, and most of the bars and restaurants are also located here. Rooms are spacious and stateside-like and the rooms in the main building are similar, except for the view. Most have excellent ocean views, some look out over the harbor (which is also pretty), and a few get only sky and parking lot. Garden View rooms are larger than Ocean View rooms, but have no balcony. The top level consists of 22 two-story suites. The pool complex, which overlooks the harbor, has cascading waterfalls, fountains, jacuzzis, and a swim-up bar. You'll want to choose Frenchman's Reef if you want to be close to just about everything and don't mind not being right on the beach.

Morning Star Resort is the place to stay if you want to fall out of your bed onto the beach. The 96 rooms here are in a series of small three-story buildings that line the beach and are either oceanfront, ocean view, or garden view. Units are decorated in tropical decor and have large terraces or balconies. There are two restaurants and bars close by and a large pool right at the end of the beach. Each resort has its own check-in desk, so be sure to tell your taxi driver which resort you are checking into.

There are five restaurants, including Caesar's Ristorante, which specializes in Italian and Mediterranean cuisine, and eight bars, including a nightclub. There are tennis courts, a health spa with state-of-the-art exercise equipment and numerous therapeutic massage and skin care treatments, and a watersports center, and snorkeling, sailing, parasailing, and scuba diving trips can all be arranged. Shoppers can spend time in the on-site retail and duty-free shops, or catch the little boat that makes daily trips to Charlotte Amalie.

5 restaurants, 8 bars, room service (6 a.m.-11 p.m.), 3 pools, beach, 2 tennis courts, watersports center, health club/spa. 504 units. P.O. Box 7100, Charlotte Amalie, 00801. Res: 800-524-2000. Tel: 340-776-8500. Fax: 340-774-6249. www.marriott.vi. $175-$450, suites more.

COLONY'S POINT PLEASANT RESORT

This remarkable waterfront resort is scattered up the side of a steep hill and nestled in dense greenery. Great care has been taken not to disturb the environment. Come here if you love great views and like to walk on winding, woodsy trails. The shore is rocky and the beaches miniscule but there's a long beach next door and the pools here are superb.

You'd never know there are 134 rooms in this place. Units are in one- to four-story, red-roofed buildings discretely tucked here and there, surrounded by trees. Narrow paths (some fairly steep) and wooden walkways lead from building to building, pool to pool, to reception and the restaurants, and off into the woods. Benches and hammocks along the walks offer nice rest stops.

Units have a gracious and welcoming feel, with wide expanses of glass that show off the view. Studio, one-, and two-bedroom units are available, many with great long terraces. The higher up you are, the more spectacular the views. All have full kitchens, TVs, and air-conditioning, and comfortable furnishings make these units that you can really settle into.

The Agave Terrace restaurant is a popular dinner spot featuring seafood and the tiny and casual Bayside restaurant and bar sits on the rocky shore and is open from late morning until 8:30 p.m. Order a full breakfast at the Agave Terrace or opt for the free coffee and danish served in reception. Three spectacular pools are at different levels with different views. Amazingly, you can almost always find an empty one—people who stay here seem to be off doing things—and don't be surprised if an iguana wanders by to take a look at you while you are sunning. The watersports center offers complimentary windsurfers, snorkel equipment, little sailboats and, once a week, an introductory scuba lesson. There's a small exercise room and a tennis court.

This is a resort that wants to make life easy for you. You can have a free car for up to four hours a day (there's a small insurance charge). There are shuttles to Charlotte Amalie and to Red Hook (five minutes away and a good place to get groceries) and evening shuttles to popular restaurants around the island. There's an activities desk, a gift shop with sodas and snacks, and a lending library. You can easily walk to the Renaissance Grand Beach Resort, which is next door, for a long beach and several more restaurants and bars.

Restaurant, bar, 3 pools, tennis court, shop. Special packages. 134 units. 6600 Smith Bay Rd., 00802. Res: 800-524-2300 or 800-777-1700. Tel: 340-775-7200. Fax: 340-776-5694. www.pointpleasantresort.com. $185-$290.

ELYSIAN BEACH RESORT

What makes this spot special is the combination of excellent service, spacious and contemporary units (many with full kitchens), appealing private grounds, and being perhaps the most central location on the east end of St. Thomas. It's just a mile to the little town of Red Hook and numerous restaurants are within a five- to ten-minute drive.

Four- and five-story buildings, all the color of ripe peaches, are clustered together on a steep hillside that sweeps down to a long crescent of beach. The 180 deluxe rooms and suites look out past beautifully manicured grounds to a picturesque harbor and St. James Island in the distance. Units are bright and spacious with comfortable white-washed rattan furnishings, white tile floors, and pale pastel fabrics. The suites have full kitchens and extra-spacious terraces, and some are duplexes with spiral staircases leading to a second-floor bedroom loft and a second private balcony. All rooms have air-conditioning, TVs, and VCRs.

The free-form swimming pool has a waterfall (check out the secret underwater bench behind it) and the beach is a half-moon of glistening white sand. Sailboats, kayaks, pedal boats, beach floats, snorkel gear, and even an introductory scuba lesson are complimentary. Parasailing, dive and snorkel trips, sailing excursions, boat rentals, and sport fishing trips can be arranged. A tennis court, a health and fitness center, and a large boutique round out the plentiful facilities.

The open-air Palm Court restaurant is a pleasant stop for breakfast, lunch, and dinner. There's a very casual restaurant down on the beach that serves lunch and early dinner. Guests gather around the piano bar Monday, Wednesday, and Saturday evenings to listen to piano music from 7 p.m. to 10 p.m. and the thatched-roof beach bar turns out frozen specialty drinks all day long. Friday evenings, there is often a steel drum band.

You never have to leave the property, but if you feel like venturing outside the Elysian, you'll find that you are in one of the best east end locations. Good restaurants are close by in virtually every direction and the town of Red Hook is practically around the corner.

Restaurant, bar, pool, tennis court, health club and fitness center, watersports center, shop. 180 units. Cowpet Bay, 6800 Estate Nazareth, St. Thomas, 00802. Res: 800-753-2554. Tel: 340-775-1000. Fax: 340-776-0910. $200-$375.

23

PAVILIONS AND POOLS

You'll love this place if you have ever dreamed about being able to fall out of bed into your own very private pool—one that you can swim in by the light of the sun or the full moon. It's not a full-service resort and it doesn't have a beach (although one is a short walk away) but it does have complete indoor and outdoor privacy.

Pavilions and Pools is nestled on the east end of St. Thomas on a hill just above Sapphire Beach. Two long, rather ordinary-looking buildings house rows of delightfully comfortable and very private apartments, each with its own personal swimming pool.

A fenced-in terrace around the pool affords true privacy. All you can see are trees and sky and you are visible to no one, except perhaps a passing bird. You are free to swim or float as naked as you wish, under the noonday sun or gazing up at the midnight stars. These pools are literally right next to both the living room and bedroom area and you can actually step right into the pool from either room, or sit at the edge of the room and dangle your legs in the water.

The units (and pools) come in two sizes. The International features a 20' x 14' pool and 1400 square feet of living space. The Caribbean has a 16' x 18' pool and 1200 square feet of living space. All units have an air-conditioned bedroom, living room, and full kitchen, plus a shower nestled against a sunken garden. The larger units have a dining area and walk-in closets and a bigger shower-garden area. All units have a TV and VCR.

This is a wonderful place to completely relax. An informal little brick and stone honor bar is open from 8 a.m. to 9 p.m. Continental breakfast is served here and so is dinner every night but Friday. It's for guests only, and the menu is very limited (one or two entrees are prepared each evening—it might be BBQ ribs or steak or chicken). If you feel like cooking, leave the dishes and don't feel guilty. Doing dirty dishes is included in the housekeeping service (do leave a nice tip if you leave a lot of kitchen messes). There's a video library if you feel like watching a movie. Many restaurants (and an excellent grocery store) are five minutes away and there's a daily shuttle into Charlotte Amalie. Long-time manager Tammy Waters does a superb job of making sure everyone has a great stay.

Continental breakfast included in the rate, dinner restaurant with limited menu, private pools. Excellent special packages. 25 units, all with pools. 6400 Estate Smith Bay Rd., 00802. Res: 800-524-2001. Tel: 340-775-6110. Fax: 340-775-6110. www.pavilionsandpools.com. $180-$275.

RENAISSANCE GRAND BEACH RESORT

This busy and popular 290-room, full-service resort sweeps down a manicured hillside to a long strip of beach. It specializes in watersports and offers just about every activity you can imagine, above the water and below.

This is the northernmost of the string of resorts that line the east end of St. Thomas. It's set among beautifully manicured lawns bordered by tropical greenery and colorful flowers. Rooms and suites are in a series of two- to four-story grey buildings that stretch up a hill back from the beach. Rooms are spacious with wide balconies and most have great views of the water and of nearby St. John and the British Virgin Islands. Units have air-conditioning, small refrigerators, televisions, and truly excellent pillows.

The beach is a 1000-foot-long arc of white sand with a complete watersports program: jet skis, windsurfers, pedal boats, and snorkeling. The Chris Sawyer Dive Center and a boutique are at the far end of the beach. The larger of the two swimming pools is just off the beach along with a pool bar and a snack bar. The more quiet, more private pool is hidden away from the beach, across from Smuggler's Steak and Seafood Grill.

There are three restaurants. Smuggler's Steak and Seafood Grill is back among the palm trees and is the place to go for a fancier dinner and also for the popular Sunday brunch and the famous "make-your-own" 12-foot-long Bloody Mary bar. Bay Winds is just off the beach and offers casual dining for breakfast, lunch, and dinner, plus a long bar facing the water. The adjoining Palm Cafe snack bar has light fare and the poolside Palm Bar cranks out tropical drinks.

In the reception building, you'll find a knowledgeable concierge who can assist with everything from baby-sitters to menus of various restaurants. There's also a tiny store selling liquor and snacks (the hotel's answer to mini-bars) and, on the second level, a hair salon, and two terrific W. H. Smith shops, one full of superb resortwear (dresses, bathing suits, cover-ups, beach bags) and the other offering a great selection of magazines, newspapers, T-shirts, and sundries. Service is friendly and prompt, and it's a pleasure to stay here.

3 restaurants, 3 bars, 24-hour room service, 2 pools, beach, 6 tennis courts, fitness center, massage, beauty salon, 2 gift shops. Special packages. 290 units. Smith Bay Rd., P.O. Box 8267, St. Thomas, 00801. Res: 800-468-3571. Tel: 340-775-1510. Fax: 340-775-2185. www.renaissancehotels.com. $155-$445, suites more.

25

RITZ-CARLTON, ST. THOMAS

There is no question that this is the most luxurious resort in the U.S. Virgin Islands and one of the best in all of the Caribbean. When you want exceptional comfort and service, superb meals in elegant settings, and stunning views, this is definitely the place to come.

A gracious brick driveway lined with a profusion of brilliantly-colored tropical flowers leads to the formal entrance of this replica of a Venetian Palace. It's not until you reach the registration desk, though, that your gaze is drawn to a window and you get your first real look at this magnificent resort—Italian villa-style buildings lead out to a point on the right and, below you, sweeping down to an exquisite pool, is what can only be called "perfect planting." Walkways head hither and yon between these beautifully-manicured lawns and blossoming trees.

The rooms are plush and very civilized. Upholstered sofas provide a comfortable seating area. Wide French doors open onto a very private bougainvillaea-lined balcony when you want sunlight and views. Heavy draperies shut out light when you want to sleep. In some rooms the comfortable king size bed is perfectly positioned so you can lie and look straight out at the view if you want. (A few rooms have two queens.) The pillows are excellent. There are TVs with in-room movies. The marble bathrooms are quite spacious and luxurious for the Caribbean, with heavy chrome bath fixtures, piles of ultra-plush towels, and great water pressure.

The air-conditioned Dining Room, Ritz-Carlton's signature restaurant, is predictably elegant (jacket or collared shirt required on-season) and the Cafe serves fine cuisine in a more casual atmosphere and is open for breakfast, lunch, and dinner. For barefoot dining, Iguana's, out by the pool, is the place to congregate for breakfast and lunch. Each restaurant has a bar and guests gather in the Florentine Room to shoot pool, smoke cigars, and drink brandy.

The pool is stunning, with a view that looks out over its "disappearing edge" to distant islands. There is a half-mile of beach, three tennis courts, a health club and spa, and shopping shuttles to Charlotte Amalie. Several upscale boutiques sell sportswear and a 53' catamaran goes on daily sails.

3 restaurants, 3 bars, 24-hour room service, pool, beach, 3 tennis courts, health club and spa, several shops. Special packages. 152 units. 6900 Great Bay, 00802. Res: 800-241-3333. Tel: 340-775-3333. Fax: 340-775-4444. www.ritzcarlton.com. $250-$575, suites more.

26

SAPPHIRE BEACH RESORT AND MARINA

A half-mile crescent of white sand, turquoise waters, and a view of St. John and the British Virgin Islands in the distance provide an exquisite setting for this casual, full-service resort that is popular with families.

Don't worry that the entrance is less than grand. A dirt driveway swings down through somewhat unkempt foliage to an unassuming yellow building and other than the distant view of islands, there isn't much to see. But walk through to the other side and you're bound to like the superb beach and stunning view.

The beach here is exceptionally wide and accommodations are in several tin-roofed, four-story buildings at the far edge of the sand. Units are casually and simply decorated but extremely comfortable. The entrance leads past a bathroom through the bedroom to a living room with a sleeper sofa and seating arrangement, a dining table, and a full kitchen along one wall. A wide balcony that is perfect for lounging day and night looks across the beach to distant islands. TVs are hidden in rattan armoires. All units are air-conditioned.

Tables at the Seagrape, the main restaurant, sit under umbrellas on a terrace overlooking the beach and open to the breezes. Nearby, on the same terrace is a circular beach bar, which is open day and night and which is the site for weekend entertainment. The Steakhouse at the Point is open for dinner on-season. You'll find a casual bar and restaurant out by the pool.

The half-mile-long beach curves around the bay in a sweeping arc and is good for walking as well as sunning. Hammocks are strung here and there. While the two ends of the beach are less crowded and it can be possible to find a spot by yourself under a sea grape tree, the center of the beach tends to be busy, particularly at the volleyball court and around the watersports center, which offers complimentary snorkeling, sunfish sailing, and windsurfing. There is a charge for parasailing and renting waverunners. The watersports center can also arrange sport fishing and sailing trips. An on-site full-service PADI dive center offers certification programs and diving trips. Handcrafted stone walls and a glassy waterfall separate the two tiers of the gorgeous pool which is out on a point at the end of the beach. Guest services offers a huge array of activities at the resort—crab races, sand castle contests, tennis clinics—and also around the island, from sunset sails to tours of St. Thomas.

3 restaurants, 2 bars, pool, beach, 4 tennis courts. Special packages. 171 units. P.O. Box 8088, 00802. Res: 800-524-2090. Tel: 340-775-6100. Fax: 340-775-2403. www.usvi.net/hotel/sapphire. $225-$500.

27

WYNDHAM SUGAR BAY RESORT

This is an absolutely all-inclusive, full-service resort and everything really is included. Eat, drink, play tennis, go windsurfing, bring your children in the summer—all at no additional charge.

Staying here is almost like going on a cruise but knowing you don't have to worry about getting seasick. Virtually everything is included in the price of your room: all meals and snacks (and you can eat all day long here), all drinks including wine, champagne, and premium brand liquors (Absolut vodka, Johnny Walker scotch, etc.) during bar hours (which are extensive); use of all non-motorized boats; daily activities; classes; and evening entertainment.

Rooms are in two tiers of rather imposing three-story buildings that crown a small hill. They are large and comfortably furnished and have private balconies. Some have simply stunning views of nearby islands, others catch the bay, and others look out to the pool and up into the hills. Rooms all have ceiling fans and air-conditioning, a coffee maker and small refrigerator, and a TV with in-room movies. Depending on how much you intend to get for your money, however, you may never be in your room.

From 7 a.m until 11 p.m. there's always food available. The Manor House (reservations necessary and a "Caribbean smart" dress code) serves a buffet breakfast, for dinner switches back and forth from a la carte to themed buffets, and also offers a late night (until 11 p.m.) menu. The casual, poolside Mangrove restaurant offers a different lunch buffet daily and themed dinner buffets. Hot dogs, hamburgers, grilled fish, and other goodies are available at a poolside grill from noon to 5 p.m. You can always find a bar open from 11 a.m. to 1 a.m. Nightly entertainment features live bands, karaoke, and DJs.

It's a steep drop (via stairs or elevator) down to the pool and beach area. A swinging bridge crosses over free-form pools with great waterfalls you can swim under and hide behind. There's a small beach and for no additional charge, you can snorkel, sunfish, windsurf, take out a Hobie Cat or a catamaran, or just lie back and relax. (You can also walk around the rocks to the trail to the Renaissance beach if you feel like a walk). Scheduled activities run day and night (power walks, bingo, movies). Castaways is a superb shop in the lobby. If you find time to leave, Red Hook is minutes away.

2 restaurants, 3 bars, 3 pools with waterfalls, beach, 5 tennis courts, basketball, beach volleyball, fitness center, shop. 300 units. 6500 Estate Smith Bay, 00802. Res: 800-WYNDHAM (800-996-3426). Tel: 340-777-7100. Fax: 340-777-7200. www.travelweb.com. $360-$580.

RENTING A ST. THOMAS VILLA OR CONDO

Some people think renting a villa is incredibly expensive, that villas are truly luxurious and only for the "rich and famous." Actually they are available in a wide range of sizes and prices, and many are competitive with resort rates.

Villas are wonderful if you would like the convenience of a house—privacy, ability to walk from one room to another, space, a full kitchen. Some families love them because everyone can "hang out" together around their own private pool (or even in the kitchen, just the way they do at home).

Off-season, special lower rates and packages make even big fancy villas very affordable, especially if several couples share in the cost or you have a large family. Smaller villas can be a romantic way to celebrate an anniversary. One of the advantages to renting a villa on St. Thomas is location. While most resorts are located on the east and south sides of the island, villas are scattered all over. Many are near beautiful Magen's Bay and others are high up in the hills, with unbeatable, airplane-like views of neighboring islands.

*A great source for villas is **Island Destinations**. Call for a color brochure with photographs of the insides and outside of all the available villas. They also represent upscale resorts in the Caribbean.* 1875 Palmer Ave., Larchmont, NY 10538. Tel: 800-942-5499. Fax: 914-833-3318. www.islanddestinations.com.

*Another good source is the Island Marketplace and Vacation Rental Guide in the back of each issue of **Caribbean Travel & Life**. Check your newsstand or call 800-588-1689.*

29

STUFF PEOPLE USUALLY WISH THEY HAD KNOWN SOONER

CHARLOTTE AMALIE AND A BEACH
If you are staying near downtown Charlotte Amalie, an easy and enjoyable way to reach a beach is to catch "The Reefer," the little ferry that runs between the waterfront and Marriott Frenchman's Reef Hotel (which is on Morningstar Beach). The ferry leaves from the downtown waterfront. You can usually find it across from Bumpa's and Down Island Trader. The trip takes about 15 minutes and costs $4. *See page 140 for schedules.*

CHARLOTTE AMALIE HOSPITALITY LOUNGE
When you want an indoor pay phone, a rest room, a place to sit down, or tourist information, head to the Hospitality Lounge. You can also leave luggage here for a small fee per bag. It's in the Grand Hotel complex across from Emancipation Park. This place is run entirely by volunteers, so please leave a small donation if you can.

STATESIDE PAPERS
You can get current editions of *The New York Times,* the *New York Post,* the *Washington Post,* the *Miami Herald,* and the *Wall Street Journal* every morning at Island Newsstand in the Grand Hotel complex downtown.

ST. JOHN AND THE BRITISH VIRGIN ISLANDS
It is really easy to head over to one of these islands for a day and it can be a great adventure, so build it into your schedule. Each island is different, so choose the one you think you'll like the most or see them all with a group.

THINGS TO NOTICE ON ST. THOMAS

The tourists who didn't pack a carry-on.
They are the ones strolling the beach in their
Brooks Brothers' suits.

The green flash
as the sun settles into the Caribbean.

Shooting stars and satellites—if you gaze at the night
sky for fifteen minutes, you'll see at least one.
Guaranteed.

How close the stars look—as if you could just
reach out and touch them.

Phosphorus lighting up the night sea.

The delightful donkey at Drake's Seat.

Iguanas—they are a little ugly but they know
how to relax.

Beautiful hummingbirds hanging around
the hibiscus blossoms.

DID YOU KNOW?

❑St. Thomas is on the same geologic shelf as the British Virgin Islands and Puerto Rico. It is thought that several times in the last 60 million years you could probably have walked from one island to another on dry land.

❑St. Thomas is 18 degrees north of the equator.

❑If you headed straight east, you'd cross the British Virgin Islands, the island of Anguilla, and then, 3,000 miles later, the Cape Verde Islands off the coast of North Africa.

❑If you walked along St. Thomas' curvy coastline until you got back to where you started, you would have walked almost 60 miles.

❑The turpentine tree is distinctive-looking, with red-orange bark. It's sometimes called the "tourist tree" because its skin is constantly peeling.

❑The machineel tree can be a real pain. It bears small green apples which are poisonous. Its sap and bark can cause painful blistering that feels just like a bad burn. Don't even stand under the tree in a rain—water dripping from the leaves will burn your skin.

❑The reason there are so many stairs outside in Charlotte Amalie is that the Danes laid out plans for the city back in Denmark and thought the land was flat. When it came time to build, everywhere it was just too steep to put a street, they had to build a stairway instead.

CHAPTER 2

GREAT ST. THOMAS RESTAURANTS

"Part of the secret of success in life
is to eat what you like and
let the food fight it out inside."

—*Mark Twain*

GREAT ST. THOMAS RESTAURANTS

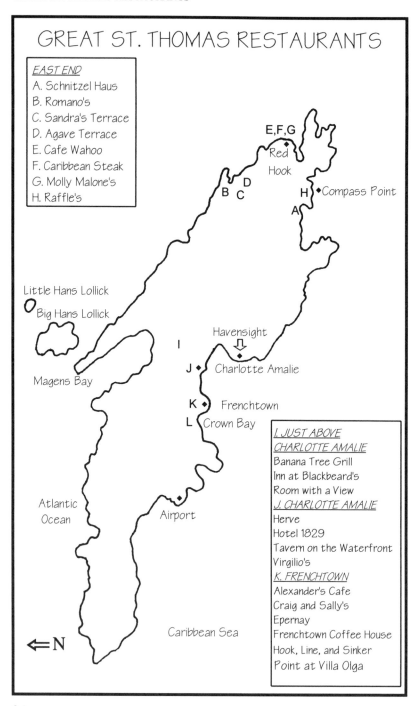

EAST END
A. Schnitzel Haus
B. Romano's
C. Sandra's Terrace
D. Agave Terrace
E. Cafe Wahoo
F. Caribbean Steak
G. Molly Malone's
H. Raffle's

E,F,G
Red
Hook
D
B C
H ◆Compass Point
A

Little Hans Lollick
Big Hans Lollick

Havensight

I

J ◆ Charlotte Amalie

Magens Bay

K ◆ Frenchtown

L Crown Bay

Atlantic
Ocean

Airport

Caribbean Sea

⇐N

I. JUST ABOVE
CHARLOTTE AMALIE
Banana Tree Grill
Inn at Blackbeard's
Room with a View
J. CHARLOTTE AMALIE
Herve
Hotel 1829
Tavern on the Waterfront
Virgilio's
K. FRENCHTOWN
Alexander's Cafe
Craig and Sally's
Epernay
Frenchtown Coffee House
Hook, Line, and Sinker
Point at Villa Olga

GREAT ST. THOMAS RESTAURANTS

St. Thomas is a sophisticated island and has many great restaurants. Some are elegant and some are casual. Some are air-conditioned and indoors and some are open to the Caribbean breezes and look out at great nighttime views. There are many highly-skilled chefs on St. Thomas and you can expect to sample some of the best food anywhere. You will find all kinds of cuisine—Italian, German, Continental, Greek, Spanish, and West Indian. Local fish to look for on the menu include wahoo, mahi mahi, swordfish, and tuna.

Most restaurants on St. Thomas are either clustered in or above Charlotte Amalie and in Frenchtown (which is just around the corner from Charlotte Amalie), or they are out on the east end of the island in or near Red Hook. In the evening it's about a 20-25 minute ride between the two areas. One-way taxi fare is $5.50 to $8.50 per person for two or more people. The same taxi that takes you to your restaurant will pick you up also, if you want. The restaurants described below are open seven days a week for lunch and dinner unless otherwise noted. Bear in mind that some places will close for lunch off-season, so it is a good idea to call.

DOWNTOWN CHARLOTTE AMALIE RESTAURANTS

HOTEL 1829 RESTAURANT

Long considered one of St. Thomas' best restaurants, the Hotel 1829 offers a sophisticated menu in a refined and peaceful setting. Elegantly-set tables line the outdoor terrace of this historic landmark. The breezes are soft and the lights of Charlotte Amalie sparkle through the trees. The menu runs the gamut— perhaps pecan-crusted brie or lobster bisque to start, then grilled swordfish and shrimp, mustard-crusted rack of lamb, or one of the many nightly specials like peppered N.Y. strip with smoked gouda and wild mushrooms, or blackened tuna with sundried tomato puree. The tableside wilted spinach salad (for two) and the dessert souffles (chocolate, Grand Marnier, and strawberry) are outstanding house specialties. Service is excellent and if you are in the mood for something special, there's Sevruga and Beluga caviar, a humidor of fresh cigars, and a variety of ports, aged rums, and calvadoes. *Reservations necessary for dinner. Closed Sun. 340-776-1829. Government Hill. $$-$$$.*

35

HERVE

Dramatic floor-to-ceiling windows capture a stunning view of Charlotte Amalie and the harbor at this delightful hillside restaurant. Relax in air-conditioned comfort and enjoy some of the island's finest cuisine. Although the menu is not traditionally French, it is definitely inspired by the French owners. Tables are well-spaced and elegantly set and this is the place to come for appetizers such as pistachio-crusted brie, warm smoked quail, and escargot. Superb dinner choices include coquille St. Jacques with lobster as well as scallops, black-sesame-crusted tuna, lamb chops stuffed with spinach, and roasted breast of duck. For dessert, try the little chocolate cups brimming with berries or the rich creme caramel. The wine list is excellent. Check out the black-and-white photos of St. Thomas in gas lamp and horse-and-buggy days. *See page 78 for lunch description. Reservations a good idea for dinner. 340-777-9703. Government Hill. $$-$$$.*

TAVERN ON THE WATERFRONT

This upstairs, air-conditioned restaurant is a welcome retreat from the hustle and bustle below. A cathedral ceiling gives a feeling of space and windows along the front wall look out across the harbor with cruise ships docked in the distance and sailboats bobbing about. An amusing trompe l'oeil painting on one wall looks like a window looking west along Waterfront Highway, but it can't be real because there is absolutely no traffic! Start with a delicious appetizer, such as tempura soft shell crab or Shabu Shabu, carpaccio that you dip in a very hot sauce. Move on to salmon margarita, or a mixed grill, or spicy pork loin stuffed with apples and mashed potatoes. Save room for bread pudding with a Grand Marnier sauce. Plates here look like works of art. *See page 79 for lunch description. Reservations a must for dinner. Closed Sun., Sat. lunch. 340-776-4328. Waterfront Hwy. at Royal Dane Mall. $$-$$$.*

VIRGILIO'S

Exceptional northern Italian cuisine is served indoors in an elegant, intimate atmosphere. Walk into this dark and cozy restaurant and the rest of the world melts away. Two-story exposed brick walls are hung with a marvelous mix of all sizes of framed paintings and prints. Although tables are quite close together, in most cases, once seated, you forget you have neighbors. The menu offers everything from veal saltimboca to chicken cacciatore, filet mignon, and capellini with a fresh tomato sauce, plus several daily specials. If what you want is not on the menu, do ask. The extensive wine list includes inexpensive wines, but if you feel like splurging you can always order the Biondi-Santi Brunello Reserva 1945 for $2,500. Don't leave without trying a Virgilio's Cappuccino. *See page 79 for lunch description. Reservations a must. Closed Sun. 340-776-4920. Stortvaer Gade, between Main and Back St. $$-$$$.*

RESTAURANTS JUST ABOVE CHARLOTTE AMALIE

BANANA TREE GRILL

St. Thomas restauranteurs Liz and Jerry Buckalew owned Entre Nous, one of St. Thomas's most famous restaurants, for over 20 years and now they have replaced it with this appealing, somewhat more casual venture. This restaurant, one of the highest around, is on a broad terrace open to the Caribbean breezes, and it looks down on all of Charlotte Amalie and the harbor. At night the view of the twinkling lights down below and in the hills is simply magical. In fact, one of the great sights here is seeing a big full moon come rising up from behind the hills of St. Thomas. Dine on garlic-lime mahi mahi, sesame-seared tuna, N.Y. strip with your choice of wonderful sauces, a light vegetable medley over spaghettini, or mango barbequed chicken. Mussels, escargot, bruschetta, and conch chowder are tasty starter choices. There's a cozy little bar just inside the entrance. *Reservations necessary. Closed Mon. 340-776-4050. Bluebeard's Castle on Bluebeard Hill. $$-$$$.*

INN AT BLACKBEARD'S CASTLE RESTAURANT

This peaceful spot sits up on a hill overlooking Charlotte Amalie and is open to the soft Caribbean breezes. The view at night is very romantic, with the lights of downtown shimmering in the distance and soft breezes in the air. The menu is Caribbean-inspired and highly creative and the results are superb. Try the "fungi" polenta with poached conch or the Caribbean vegetable soup for a starter. Next consider the christophine-spinach cannelloni with roasted bell pepper sauce or the roasted rack of lamb with tamarind barbecue sauce or the spit-roasted duck with Cruzan-rum ginger sauce. The lighter lunch menu features soups, salads, and grilled fish and is equally creative. *No lunch Sat. Reservations necessary. 340-776-1234. Blackbeard's Castle. $$-$$$.*

ROOM WITH A VIEW

The decor is swanky 1940s and the view is stunning at this appealing wine bar and bistro which looks out over Charlotte Amalie. A dramatic floor-to-ceiling window at the far end of the room frames a spectacular view of town, the harbor, and the hills beyond. Sunsets here are gorgeous. You can see planes approaching and leaving the airport and at night you can watch the planes' headlights and gaze out at the glittering lights of Charlotte Amalie. The room itself is quite dark, with a little lamp on each table. There's a wine list (by the glass or bottle) and daily wine specials. The conch fritters, crab crepe, French onion soup, and warm brie almondine make good appetizers. For a main course, try the excellent lasagna, Creole shrimp, chicken marsala, or one of the fresh catches of the day. Ice cream sundaes are a specialty. *Late night menu to 1 a.m. Closed Sun. 340-774-2377. Bluebeard's Castle, Bluebeard Hill. $$.*

FRENCHTOWN RESTAURANTS

ALEXANDER'S CAFE

Excellently-prepared German and Austrian cuisine is served side-by-side with grilled fresh fish, excellent pasta, and even Vietnamese dishes at this stylish, sophisticated spot. The walls are pink, the furnishings are lacquer black, the tablecloths are crisp and white, and the overall effect is striking. This is a very small restaurant with a superb chef, a classy atmosphere, and a remarkably varied menu. You can come here for excellent, authentic weiner schnitzel or jaeger schnitzel (veal in a mushroom cream sauce). You can have pasta with several excellent sauces including a meat sauce and a quite good pesto, or you can have Pan Thai chicken with wilted spinach over a bed of linguini. You can also dine on grilled tuna, or Vietnamese style sliced N.Y. strip, or Cuban chicken with black bean salsa. *Reservations are a good idea for dinner. Closed Sun. 340-774-4349. Frenchtown Mall. $$-$$$.*

CRAIG AND SALLY'S

Two owners who really care, a great (albeit extremely eclectic) menu, and excellent food served in a casual but cosmopolitan atmosphere make this place worth coming back to again and again. There are seascape murals on the walls, five or six different dining areas, and comfortable low lighting. Craig and Sally love to run a restaurant and it shows. Nobody cares if you just want to order the shredded pork-cheddar cheese quesadilla appetizer. In fact, the wait-staff will tell you it's big and caution you from ordering anything else. The inspired and lengthy menu changes nightly and bears thorough investigation. One night the filet mignon might be stuffed with Danish blue cheese; the next night it might be served atop garlic-roasted/smoked mozarella mashed potatoes. One night you might find veal scaloppini with fried eggplant slices and a tomato-vodka alfredo sauce; the next night it might be with hot Italian sausage with an Italian grappa sauce. Shrimp, swordfish, pasta, lamb, veal—you'll find it all, prepared in wonderful ways. Sooner or later you'll notice that crates of wine are stacked here and there all over the place. Craig is the wine connoisseur and likes to offer ones that are truly unusual. Check and see what he's got when you're on the island. There's a large, comfortable bar also. *Reservations are a must in season. Closed Mon.-Tues., no lunch Sat.-Sun. 340-777-9949. Frenchtown Mall. $$.*

EPERNAY

Small tables run along one side of this tiny, dark, and sophisticated wine bar and bistro with a classy decor. Hung from the ceiling are green shades, which hover just above the tables, giving off an intimate glow. The menu choices are quite varied. Have a warm spinach salad with blue cheese or a Mediterranean caesar, or try a roasted vegetable, Asian, or Southwestern wrap. There are several good pizza choices, particularly the vegetarian pizza with eggplant and roasted tomatoes. There's a large assortment of sushi. Entrees include angel hair pommodoro, pan-roasted chicken, and sea bass with bok choy, miso, and sticky rice. Or just have one after another of the tempting appetizers: quesadilla with pepper jack cheese, tuna tartare, champagne peppercorn pate with capers and onions, a board of cheeses with roasted garlic, or the Epernay Platter with smoked salmon, brie, and pate. *Closed Sun., no lunch Sat. 340-774-5348. Frenchtown Mall. $-$$.*

POINT AT VILLA OLGA
Come here for true al fresco dining. This restaurant is right at the end of a point and there are no walls, just a tin roof and a broad terrace and nicely-spaced tables. The view looks out to East Gregorie Channel and Water and Hassel Islands. The menu is basically Continental and features prime rib and grilled steaks, chicken, and fresh local fish. There is also an enormous salad bar which you can have as a full meal if you so desire. There's an inside bar and lounge with pleasant seating arrangements and a small terrace also. *No lunch. 340-774-4262. Villa Olga. $$.*

FRENCHTOWN COFFEE HOUSE
The atmosphere here is welcoming, with Oriental rugs on the floor and photographs and artwork on the walls. Stop here for coffee, espresso, bagels, and breakfast muffins. You can also step into the deli next door for a sandwich and eat it while perusing the latest editions of the *Wall Street Journal* and *The New York Times. 340-776-7211. Frenchtown Mall.*

HOOK, LINE, AND SINKER
A truly great restaurant masquerading as a coffee shop might be the best way to describe this all-day dining spot. The building is attractive weathered wood outside, and inside it's an upscale coffee shop, with booths along the walls, simple tables, and a counter where you can eat. Windows are open to tropical breezes and you can see pelicans diving for food. This is the kind of place that you could come to seven days in a row for breakfast, lunch, and dinner and have something different and it would all be good. Hamburgers (available lunch and dinner) are great but so are the lunchtime sandwiches. There's a terrific Reuben and also a great Black Russian (pumpernickel plus corned beef, turkey, and coleslaw). For dinner, choose pasta dishes, or fresh fish such as grilled swordfish or pecan-coated red snapper, or the London broil with homemade mashed potatoes. Check the blackboard for great daily specials like the roast turkey platter or the great Chili Taco Salad. *Open 7 a.m., except Sun. when it's brunch only 10 a.m.-2:30 p.m. 340-776-9708. Frenchtown. $-$$.*

EAST END RESTAURANTS

AGAVE TERRACE

Dining here is on a little terrace or in a breezy room with open walls. Fish is the specialty at this hillside spot. It can be extremely busy, especially on-season. Check out the blackboard as you walk onto the terrace entrance of this popular seafood restaurant. The specialty here is fresh fish and the blackboard reports the day's choice of catches—four or five fresh fish daily—prepared grilled, pan fried, blackened, baked, or batter fried. If you've spent the day catching your own on a deep-sea fishing trip, they'll be happy to prepare your catch. The menu also includes grilled steaks, a grilled chicken breast, a number of steak choices, and several chicken dish choices including linguini with chicken. The view from the terrace and the bar is truly spectacular. It looks out toward St. John and the British Virgin Islands. *Reservations necessary. Closed Mon. No lunch. 340-775-4142. East End on Smith Bay Road at Point Pleasant Resort. $$.*

CAFE WAHOO

A long, open hallway leads out to this appealing al fresco restaurant, where tables are set on a broad terrace overlooking the American Yacht Harbor Marina. Come here to enjoy the soft ocean breezes and dine on superbly-cooked fresh fish like mahi mahi, wahoo, and tuna. Try the very spicy Jamaican rubbed wahoo or the tuna, cooked rare and coated in sesame seeds. A rich bouillabaisse, a hearty and flavorful Mediterranean fish chowder, is the house specialty. *Reservations a good idea in season. No lunch. 340-775-6350. Red Hook. $$-$$$.*

CARIBBEAN STEAK HOUSE AND SALOON

Crowds flock here day and night to enjoy the excellent cuisine and relax in the tropical atmosphere. Twelve foot high wooden sculptures of banana trees and palm trees, plus mirrors and colorful fish mobiles give the restaurant a light and airy Caribbean feeling. However, despite the decor, this a true steak house and saloon. Come here for superb top sirloin, rib eye, New York strip, and filet mignon, all available in various size cuts and, if you want, rubbed with green peppercorn or habenero pepper marinade. Prime rib and Danish baby back ribs are also featured. The extensive menu also includes stir-fry dishes, roasted chicken, lobster and grilled local fish, and pastas. Appetizers such as seafood chowder, conch chowder, chili, Caesar salad, conch fritters, and calamari are offered. On the lunch menu and cafe menu (served until 4:00 a.m.), you'll find Philly cheesesteaks, hamburgers, BLTs, pulled pork sandwiches, and a quarter pound hot dog. *340-775-7060. American Yacht Harbor, Red Hook. $-$$$.*

MOLLY MALONE'S

Come here for breakfast, lunch, and back again for dinner. This spot is extremely casual and very popular with locals day and night. It faces the American Yacht Harbor and your view is of a huge array of boats tied up at slips. There's a large, open-air bar and tables are scattered about. Despite the name, much more than Irish items are on the menu. So drop by for a fish 'n chips or shepherd's pie or a cheeseburger or a Philly cheesesteak or grilled fresh local fish or lobster or a thick steak. There is a busy bar with great island drinks. *340-775-1270. American Yacht Harbor, Red Hook. $-$$.*

RAFFLES

This old St. Thomas favorite has been around forever but it just keeps getting better. The entrance isn't much but inside you'll find a relaxing dining room with high-backed rattan chairs and lazily-rotating ceiling fans and you'll feel as if you are on a movie set. This is the place to come for fresh fish, grilled steaks, duck, vegetarian pasta, and veal. House specialties include beef Wellington, West Indian style fish in a spicy tomato sauce, mango-marinated breast of chicken, and pan-seared breast of duck with an orange glaze. The lunch menu is lighter and features hamburgers, salads, and fresh fish. Try the Sir Stamford Sling, the restaurant's signature drink and an adaptation of the famous Singapore Sling. *Reservations for dinner essential in season. Closed Mon. 340-775-6004. Compass Point Marina.*

ROMANO'S

This is **the place** on-season and reservations are a must to dine at Tony Romano's swank northern Italian restaurant. Fresh flowers are on the table and the service is professional at this slightly bright, very upscale spot. The menu is classic (and-not-so-classic, but equally delicious) northern Italian. Lingua di Bue Brasta (veal tongue) and Ossobucco are the most popular dishes here. The roasted carrot soup and the artichoke puree with mushrooms and penne (both of which aren't usually on the menu but might be a special when you are there) are superb. Look for Tony. He's usually working hard in the kitchen, but he often wanders out toward the end of the evening to greet his guests. This is one of the most popular restaurants on St. Thomas and you may have to wait a bit on-season, even with a reservation. There's a little terrace where you can have a drink but it's far more interesting to sit at the bar and check out the huge number of interesting spirits and grappas that crowd the shelves. Check out the paintings and watercolors hung along the walls. Tony finds these artists in the Dominican Republic. Cigar lovers will want to try a Tony Romano smoke, or even take some home in the handsome box. This truly is a restaurant you do not want to miss. *Closed Sun. Dinner only. 340-775-0045. Coral World Rd., Smith Bay. $$-$$$.*

SANDRA'S TERRACE

For the best conch fritters on St. Thomas, head to this large, informal, and rather busy restaurant close to Smith Bay. The specialty here is West Indian cuisine and if you haven't tried it before, well, there couldn't be a better place to start than Sandra's. The casual planting and unassuming appearance of this open-walled two-story building belie the excellent West Indian food one can find inside. Come here for the best conch on the island. Have it cooked in lime juice and butter or fried into a fritter. Or try the old wife (fish) or snapper in a spicy red sauce. Some specials are served only one day a week. If you want to try Sandra's famous kallaloo stew, you'll have to be lucky. She makes it on a whim. *Reservations suggested. No lunch Sun. 340-775-3975. On Smith Bay Road on the east end of St. Thomas. $$.*

SCHNITZEL HAUS

For authentic German cuisine you'll definitely want to dine at this popular east end eatery. The owner is German and veal is the specialty here, prepared many ways. Two of the best are the weiner schnitzel (thin slices of pounded and lightly breaded veal served with lemon slices) and the jager schnitzel (veal topped with bacon, onions, and mushrooms). *Closed Sun., Mon. No lunch. 340-776-7198. At Trawler's in Paradise near the Fish Hawk Marina. $$.*

RESTAURANT HOPPING BY BOAT

For an evening of fun, head out to Compass Point Marina and onto the Merry Ferry for an evening of restaurant hopping. Just leave your car in the parking lot and let the pilot do the driving. The little wooden ferry makes the rounds of half a dozen restaurants along Mangrove Lagoon. From sushi to seafood, from West Indian to West German, you can stop at any one of the featured restaurants for a drink or for dinner and then get back on the boat and go to yet another place. The boat makes the rounds continuously and gets back to the first stop every half hour. *Fri.-Sat. 6:00-midnight. Unlimited stops. $5 per person, including two rum drinks on board. 340-775-9500.*

SOME GREAT BAKERIES, DELIS, AND TAKE-OUT FOOD

In Charlotte Amalie
King's Caribbean Coffee Cafe *(340-776-9523)*, which is on Waterfront Highway tucked between the Green House and Blazing Photos, features many flavors of superb, freshly ground coffee (hot or cold or even frozen) and tasty pastries and rolls.

Sunshine Bakery *(340-774-6765)*, at 1 B General Gade, bakes great coconut bread, buns, and the best dumb bread on the island.

Frenchtown
Frenchtown Deli *(340-776-7211)* makes great sandwiches (create your own or choose from the list on the board), and you can buy cold sodas, a wide variety of beer and ales; cheeses; pates; knockwurst, bratwurst, and andouille sausage; various salads; and freshly-baked breads.

Red Hook
Grateful Deli *(340-775-5160)*, across from the American Yacht Harbor complex, has interesting and unusual sandwiches plus a vegetarian menu.

Haagen Dazs Bakery and Ice Cream *(340-774-7505)*, also across from the American Yacht Harbor, is hard to pass up if you have any interest in ice cream.

American Yacht Harbor Deli *(340-775-2944)* makes great traditional sandwiches—ham, tuna, roast beef.

Marina Market *(340-779-2411)* is the best market on St. Thomas and also has excellent food to go. Come and get a salad or pick up dinner for the whole family.

TAXIS AND TAXI DRIVERS

Taxis in St. Thomas can range from compact cars that hold just a few passengers, to large old station wagons that can accommodate a medium size family plus luggage, to vans and open-air safari buses that can carry close to 20 people.

It is the custom in St. Thomas (and many other islands) to fill up the taxi with people before heading off.

People from the mainland are generally "in a hurry" and can think it's a waste of their vacation time to be made to wait for other people. There is another point of view. Consider, for example, that an islander sees not filling the van as a waste of space (empty seats), a waste of fuel (making the trip twice), and lost income. Plus, what's the hurry?

TAXI TIPS

❑If you are planning to get a taxi from the airport, you'll discover that this is a good time to begin practicing your adjustment to "island time." You'll find that vans sometimes even "wait for the next plane" (which actually won't be that long, since it is probably already on the ground). Hurrying won't get you to your final destination any sooner, and since you have probably already been traveling (including waiting time) from somewhere between four and 17 hours, what's another 15 minutes? Feel and breathe the air and look around. If you are alone or with one or two others and want to head to your destination immediately, look for cab that is almost full. But the best thing to do is to go have a beer at the bar near the luggage carousel and then go get in a cab. You'll most likely find your planemates inside, waiting!

❏If you are in Charlotte Amalie and want to go to Havensight, the quickest way is to look for a fairly full van or safari bus where the driver is calling, "Back to the ship." Just hop on and tell the driver you want to go to the Havensight shops.

❏At hotels, taxis wait in line, and the hotel or doorman will fill taxis with people heading to similar destinations. This can be a good way to meet people and share information.

❏Don't be shy about taking the front seat next to the driver of your taxi. He or she will be pleased. Do buckle up. It's the law in St. Thomas, and taken very seriously.

❏If you get a chance, converse with the taxi drivers. They are generally not only kind but very interesting people. Some have lived on St. Thomas for years and can tell you stories about St. Thomas long ago. Many grew up on other Caribbean islands—Tortola in the BVI, St. Kitts, Antigua, Dominica. You'll also find out that many of the drivers have had numerous careers and lived for long periods in Hartford, Connecticut, or New York City, or Omaha.

❏If you call to have a taxi pick you up, you'll be given the number of the taxi that will come and get you. This number is also the taxi license number so it's easy to know if the taxi headed your way is actually "yours."

❏Taxi fares are regulated and the yellow *St. Thomas This Week* prints these fares. The rates in parentheses are for **each** passenger traveling to the same destination. Keep this list with you and agree on the fare with the driver before you leave. Most drivers are honest and helpful but a few do try to take advantage. The telephone number for the Taxi Lost and Found is 340-776-8294.

THE OLD AIRPORT

Travelers who first headed to St. Thomas before the early '90s remember a completely different airport— rustic perhaps, but chock full of character, and with a long, long walk to the plane. Those who know both airports might enjoy the following story.

AN ISLAND STORY

We have this friend. He lived in New York, but his heart belonged to the Virgin Islands. Several times a year for over two decades the St. Thomas Airport was the gateway to the islands he loved so much.

Each time he de-planed and made that long walk to the WWII hangar that was the terminal building, he made his first stop in what to him was a very special place.

This place had no resemblance to "Rick's" and was unquestionably the opposite of "A Clean Well-Lighted Place." This place was that weary, dark, stale-smelling Sparky's Airport Bar.

Our friend wasn't even much of a drinker, but through the years a cold Sparky's Heineken became almost sacramental. It was the phone booth where his mind slipped out of its three-piece suit and into an island shirt.

Finally, after years of just visiting, he and the wife he loved so much were actually moving—taking up residence in these beautiful islands. A dream come true, as they say.

The plane landed at dusk and it was very crowded. The man and his wife entered the terminal from a strange direction. Things seemed different in the airport. Our friend was a little disoriented so he snagged a skycap. "Sorry, how would I get to Sparky's from here?" he asked.

"Sparky's finish, mon. This terminal all new. Progress, don't ya know."

Time stopped for a second or two. Then our friend turned to his wife . . . smiled . . . and said, "That's okay. No problem. I wasn't really that thirsty."

He didn't fool her.

——Reprinted from *The Best of the Peter Island Morning Sun*

CHAPTER 3

GREAT ST. THOMAS WINE BARS, QUIET BARS, LIVELY BARS

"'Twas a woman who
drove me to drink,
and I never had
the courtesy
to thank her for it."

—*W.C. Fields*

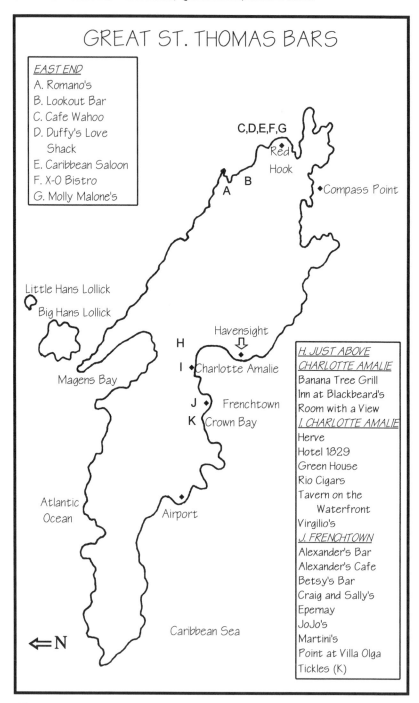

GREAT ST. THOMAS BARS

EAST END
A. Romano's
B. Lookout Bar
C. Cafe Wahoo
D. Duffy's Love Shack
E. Caribbean Saloon
F. X-O Bistro
G. Molly Malone's

C,D,E,F,G
Red Hook

B

A

◆Compass Point

Little Hans Lollick

Big Hans Lollick

Havensight

H

I ◆Charlotte Amalie

Magens Bay

J ◆ Frenchtown

K Crown Bay

Atlantic Ocean

Airport

⇐ N

Caribbean Sea

H. JUST ABOVE CHARLOTTE AMALIE
Banana Tree Grill
Inn at Blackbeard's
Room with a View
I. CHARLOTTE AMALIE
Herve
Hotel 1829
Green House
Rio Cigars
Tavern on the Waterfront
Virgilio's
J. FRENCHTOWN
Alexander's Bar
Alexander's Cafe
Betsy's Bar
Craig and Sally's
Epernay
JoJo's
Martini's
Point at Villa Olga
Tickles (K)

GREAT ST. THOMAS WINE BARS, QUIET BARS, LIVELY BARS

St. Thomas is home to classy bars, casual bars, intimate bars, and noisy bars. Some specialize in fine wines, rare single-malts, and aged ports. Some feature entertainment. What's happening when changes somewhat, depending on the season. Check St. Thomas This Week *and the* Weekend Section *in the Thursday edition of the* St. Thomas Daily News *for what is going on when you are on the island.*

CHARLOTTE AMALIE BARS

1829 BAR
This is one of the handsomest bars on St. Thomas. The room was originally an old Danish kitchen and the floors and walls are fieldstone and the ceiling is held up with rough-hewn beams. It's dark, even in the daytime, and there are comfortable tables as well as bar chairs plus backgammon boards, in case you feel like a game. Check out the blackboard for the daily selection of wines and appetizers. *Opens daily at 10 a.m. 340-776-1829. Government Hill.*

GREEN HOUSE
Crowds flock here for dancing to the Starlights every Wednesday and to D.J. music Tuesday, and Thursday through Saturday starting at 9:30 p.m. There's something happening nightly, like Margarita Monday or hula hoop contests or during sporting events (like the NBA play-offs). Check the *St. Thomas Daily News* for the latest schedules. There are pool tables and fooz-ball tables in back. This is also a restaurant and there are salads, pizzas, pastas, and barbecued ribs and chicken on the menu. *340-774-7998. Waterfront Hwy.*

HERVE
Upholstered chairs line the wide bar at this sophisticated restaurant and this is a good place to come for a quiet drink or a glass of wine. They have over 20 wines available by the glass. *340-777-9703. Government Hill.*

RIO CIGARS
This classy spot is right in the heart of the shopping district. The decor is blond wood and tile and specialties here are flavored martinis plus wines and champagnes by the glass. There's also a walk-in humidor, just in case you feel like a fine cigar. *Opens at 10 a.m. until early evening. 340-774-5877. Royal Dane Mall.*

49

TAVERN ON THE WATERFRONT

In the center of this upscale restaurant is a handsome, square, mahogany bar. If you're a beer drinker, check out their icy-cold assortment from around the world. *340-776-4328. Waterfront Hwy.*

VIRGILIO'S RESTAURANT

There's a tiny, cozy four-seat bar here. *340-776-4920. Stortvaer Gade.*

BARS JUST ABOVE CHARLOTTE AMALIE

BANANA TREE GRILL

There's a quiet bar in the back of this elegant restaurant and it's a pleasant spot to relax over a drink. And why not just make reservations and stay for dinner? *340-776-4050. Bluebeard's Castle on Bluebeard's Hill.*

INN AT BLACKBEARD'S CASTLE LOUNGE

You'll find sophisticated entertainment nightly in this delightful piano bar, starting at 7:00 p.m. Some nights it's just piano, other nights there's also guitar and sometimes vocals. You can also have an elegant snack off the late-night menu. *340-776-1234. Government Hill.*

ROOM WITH A VIEW

Floor-to-ceiling windows showcase a fabulous view of Charlotte Amalie and sunsets and nighttime scenes are wonderfully romantic. There's a long wine list, including many by the glass and a chalkboard by the bar lists daily wine and appetizer specials. There's a complete dinner menu (*see page 38*). After-dinner cordials and specialty coffees and great desserts (Godiva chocolate cheesecake, chocolate sundaes) make this an excellent end-of-the-evening stop if you've already dined next door at the Banana Tree Grill or elsewhere on the island. *Closed Sun. 340-774-2377. Bluebeard's Castle, Bluebeard Hill.*

FRENCHTOWN BARS

ALEXANDER'S BAR

This is a plain old bar—dark, smoky, sports on the TV, and you can hang out at the bar, but you can also order all the terrific food on next-door Alexander's Cafe menu as well as from a simple bar menu. *340-774-4349.*

ALEXANDER'S CAFE

The bar at the back of this classy restaurant is a popular gathering spot for locals. *Closed Sun. 340-774-4349.*

BETSY'S BAR

It's loud, crowded, and noisy at this very casual place that attracts a local crowd. They usually have live entertainment Friday and Saturday nights. *340-774-9347.*

CRAIG AND SALLY'S

This popular Frenchtown restaurant has a dark and congenial bar with seating on two sides and it fills up fast. They have a full bar but be sure to inquire about the wines by the glass. There are many, and many unusual ones. You can eat at the bar if you want. *Closed Mon.-Tues. 340-777-9949.*

EPERNAY

At this very dark and intimate bar and bistro, an interesting selection of champagnes and red and white wines of the evening are scrawled on the blackboard and there's a long list of cognacs, armagnacs, Spanish brandies, single-malt scotches, and ports by the glass. There's a small bar and cozy tables line the wall. A delightful dinner is served here, too (*see page 39*). *Closed Sun. 340-774-5348.*

JOJO'S

Dance until 4 a.m. at this nightclub that features Top 40, alternative, calypso, and salsa. *Closed Sun.-Wed. 340-714-1694.*

MARTINI'S

The action doesn't get going here until close to the witching hour, when crowds dance to rhythm and blues, classic Motown, and good old rock and roll. *Opens at 10 p.m. Music Thurs.-Sat. 340-714-2145.*

POINT AT VILLA OLGA

Inside, settle into a rattan love seat or at the comfortable bar or else head to a table outside along the narrow terrace and enjoy the soft sea breezes and twinkling nightime sky. This could be the time to try a real island drink, like a frozen strawberry margarita or an icy pina colada. *340-774-4262.*

TICKLES

It's not really in Frenchtown, but actually the next bay west, at Crown Bay Marina, which is also where you catch the ferry to Water Island (the dock is just to the side of the restaurant). This is a great open-air bar with wonderful water views and good casual fare, like burgers and fries. Locals flock here day and night and for the always popular happy hour. *340-776-1595. Crown Bay Marina.*

EAST END BARS

CAFE WAHOO

The bar is open-air and looks out to the marina and the many boats at dock. *340-775-6350. Red Hook.*

CARIBBEAN STEAK HOUSE AND SALOON

The bar is big and busy here and popular with locals. There's a great late night bar menu and often entertainment, which might be a guitarist or a saxaphonist. *340-775-7060. American Yacht Harbor. Red Hook.*

DUFFY'S LOVE SHACK

The draw at this casual, kind of funky bar is the mix of icy cold beers, tasty frozen drinks, and rock and roll music turned up high. They serve food here, too. *340-779-2080. Red Hook.*

LOOKOUT BAR

The seats are lined up to give you one of the very best views of St. John and the nearby British Virgin Islands. The sun sets in the opposite direction but sunsets are still beautiful here. If you want to be alone and avoid the crowds waiting for dinner at the popular adjoining Agave Terrace restaurant, walk past the bar to the tiny outside terrace. There's steelpan music Tuesday, Thursday, and Saturday nights. *340-775-4142. Point Pleasant Resort, Smith Bay Rd.*

MOLLY MALONE'S

The large bar is open to the breezes and the scenery is boats everywhere in the busy marina. Belly up to the bar or sit on the terrace with an icy cold beer. *340-775-1270. American Yacht Harbor.*

ROMANO'S

This narrow little bar has comfortable seats and you can spend an hour or two reading the labels on all the bottles of grappa and other interesting spirits and wines that line the wall. Or look the other way and gaze at the wonderful paintings on the walls, collected by the owner who searches out aspiring artists in the Dominican Republic. The art is for sale, if something catches your eye. *340-775-0045. Smith Bay Rd.*

X-O BISTRO

Champagnes and wines by the glass plus a full bar are the draw at this intimate spot. *340-779-2069. Red Hook.*

THE MOST ORIGINAL BAR

Puzzles wins the prize for the most original bar, certainly on St. Thomas and perhaps anywhere.

Your first thought is that you've come across a displaced Mississippi Riverboat but upon closer inspection, well ... it turns out that the owner Jack Rosen salvaged an old glass bottomed boat and turned it into this marvelous bar—adding everything from the old iron bar chairs to the flowered black carpet to the hundreds of window panes that form the walls.

Downstairs all kinds of frustrating puzzles are usually scattered along the bar (like the metal rings that you are supposed to be able to separate without a blow torch). There's a full bar here plus a number of unusual beers on tap and bottled. Jack grills hamburgers, sausages, and chicken and serves up his non-stop humorous commentary about whatever comes to mind. *Hours are irregular. Be sure to call before going. Closed Sun. 340-775-9671. Saga Haven.*

Upstairs is a delightfully charming and quite popular sushi bar. Japanese appetizers and soups are featured as well as sushi and shashimi plus Japanese beers, saki, and plum wine. *Sushi by Sato. Closed Mon.-Wed. 340-775-3352. Saga Haven.*

ST. CROIX FOR THE DAY

St. Croix sits by itself about 40 miles south of St. Thomas so it takes a bit longer to get there than it does to get to most of the other neighboring islands. However, you'll still have enough time to have fun on St. Croix, provided you have something specific in mind—you won't have time to do everything.

You can drive around the island and visit several beaches. **Olympic Car Rental** *rents cars near the dock (340-772-2000), or you can take yourself on an historic walk through downtown Christiansted (directions in the free* St. Croix This Week*).*

You can head out to the Buck Island U.S. National Park (which is different than the Buck Island just off St. Thomas), or you can ride through a rain forest on horseback. Call **Paul and Jill's Equestrian Stables** *(340-772-2880).*

You can always take a regular plane, but at the moment, there are some exciting alternatives. You can travel on a seaplane or a hydrofoil. However, please check to see what is running when you are on island. Over the last 15 years plane schedules, seaplane service, and boat transportation between these two islands has changed often.

BY PLANE
It's a 20- to 30-minute flight and planes leave from the St. Thomas airport. Round-trip fare is $100. **American Eagle** (*800-474-4884*) flies between St. Thomas and St. Croix several times daily.

BY SEAPLANE
A neat seaplane flies from the Charlotte Amalie Waterfront (at the Marine Terminal, where the ferries leave for the BVI) to right in front of the Kings Alley Hotel in Christiansted. It's a quick 17 minutes in the air. There are several morning flights and, for day-trippers, a convenient afternoon return. Fare is $110. Call **Seaborne Seaplanes** (*340-773-6442*).

BY HYDROFOIL
A 155-passenger hydrofoil runs between the St. Thomas waterfront (right across from the Holiday Inn at the Marine Terminal) and Gallows Bay on St. Croix. The trip takes an hour and fifteen minutes and is $45 each way. If you want a full day on St. Croix, you can catch the 7:15 a.m. boat over and the 5 p.m. boat back. Call **Virgin Island Hydrofoil Services** (*340-776-7417*).

Coveted Cruzan Bracelets
Look for the famous sterling silver Cruzan "hook" bracelets in jewelry stores. There are also earrings and rings. For many years you could only get these if you actually went to St. Croix, but if you run out of time, you can now buy them on St. Thomas at **Elizabeth James** in Red Hook.

ART GALLERIES

(MANY GALLERIES WILL SHIP ANYWHERE YOU WANT)

CHARLOTTE AMALIE

JONNA WHITE GALLERY. Works of local artist Jonna White (on the waterfront near Palm Passage).

CAMILLE PISSARO ART GALLERY. Originals and prints by local artists (Main Street).

CARIBBEAN PRINT GALLERY. Prints, old maps (on Main Street at A. H. Riise).

HOSPITALITY LOUNGE. Sometimes showcases works by local artists (Grand Hotel complex).

AROUND THE ISLAND

TILLET GARDENS. Art of all kinds in galleries and silk-screened fabrics and a restaurant (at Anna's Retreat).

KILNWORKS POTTERY AND ART GALLERY. A working pottery studio and work by local artists (at Smith Bay).

MANGO TANGO ART GALLERY. Caribbean art, prints, and handcrafts (at Al Cohen Mall on Raphune Hill).

REICHHOLD CENTER GALLERY. Art by local artists (at the University of the Virgin Islands).

CHAPTER 4

GREAT ST. THOMAS SHOPPING

"Whoever said money can't buy happiness
didn't know where to shop."

—Anonymous

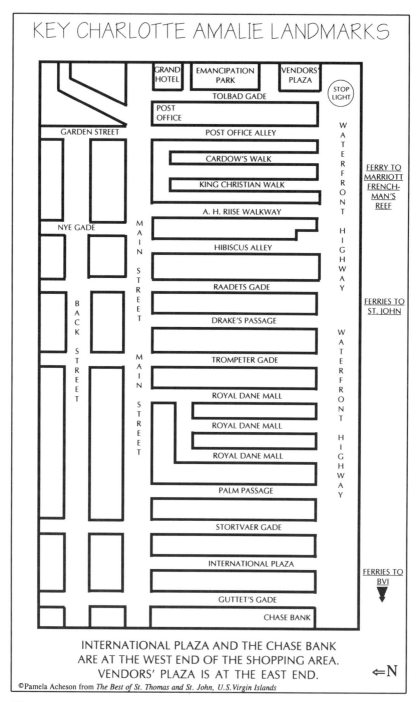

KEY CHARLOTTE AMALIE LANDMARKS

INTERNATIONAL PLAZA AND THE CHASE BANK
ARE AT THE WEST END OF THE SHOPPING AREA.
VENDORS' PLAZA IS AT THE EAST END. ⇐N

©Pamela Acheson from *The Best of St. Thomas and St. John, U.S.Virgin Islands*

SHOPPING IN CHARLOTTE AMALIE
(HAVENSIGHT AND RED HOOK STORES APPEAR AT THE END OF THIS CHAPTER)

Everyone knows that Charlotte Amalie is a world-class duty-free shopping mecca, but what no one ever points out is that there are also wonderful, original shops—intriguing stores even for people who hate to shop—with items you may never find anywhere else tucked here and there in the Charlotte Amalie alleyways.

Charlotte Amalie certainly gets its share of negative comments. People complain that it's too crowded and full of street hawkers. Well, there are hawkers and it can be very crowded when lots of cruise ships are in. Also, the place itself is somewhat confusing, and this is compounded by the throngs of people who can make it difficult to see where you are.

For some, the crowds are part of the fun. But if you want to avoid them, head downtown in mid-afternoon. Many cruise ship shoppers will have returned to their ship and the town can be quite pleasant. It also helps to go when few ships are in (check schedules in St. Thomas This Week*).*

HOW CHARLOTTE AMALIE IS ORGANIZED
Two main streets are parallel to each other and lined with shops: Waterfront Highway (which runs along the harbor) and Main Street. Numerous narrow alleys (walkways), also lined with shops, connect these two streets. Each alley has a name (often Danish, with letter combinations non-Danish speaking people can find difficult to make sense of). However, you don't really need to know these names because, although you will see these names on maps, a good number of alleys do not have identifying signs anyway.

FINDING YOUR WAY AROUND
So, how do you find anything in this rabbit warren of alleyways with non-pronounceable names that often aren't posted? Easy. People rely on landmarks—just about everything is either near the Post Office, or Vendors' Plaza, or Chase Bank. Don't be embarrassed if you can't find the store you were just in. Even locals get confused in these alleyways. See the map on page 69 to locate easily shops you want to find.

CHARLOTTE AMALIE SHOPS

The stores below are selected because they have something special to offer. Most aren't "famous" and some are places that very few people know about. They are organized alphabetically by category.

Charlotte Amalie's great duty-free stores—Columbian Emeralds, Sparky's, A.H Riise, Cardow's, and Little Switzerland (the places where you can buy diamonds and gold jewelry, gemstones, crystal, linens, watches, electronics, perfumes, cosmetics, and liquor)—aren't included below because these renowned shops are covered so thoroughly in free tourist information guides like the yellow St. Thomas This Week *and because you can't miss these large shops.*

ANTIQUES
CARSON CO. ANTIQUES
Old brick archways provide a tasteful background for these two rooms of antiquities from ancient times through the 19th century. Come to this well-laid out shop for old books (some rare), ancient coins, maps, pottery, African masks, estate and ancient jewelry, and a huge stock of Christmas ornaments. *340-774-6175. Northwest end of Royal Dane Mall.*

BOOKS, MAGAZINES, AND NEWSPAPERS
ISLAND NEWSSTAND
When you want to find out what you're missing back home, stop here for the latest issue of just about every stateside magazine imaginable plus newspapers including the *New York Post, The New York Times,* the *Miami Herald,* and the *Wall Street Journal.* You'll also find hardcovers, paperbacks, local guide books, greeting cards, and stationery supplies (scotch tape, packing tape, envelopes, pens, etc.). They sell coffee, sodas, and pastries, too. *340-774-0043. In Grand Hotel complex, across from the park.*

CARIBBEAN ITEMS
CALYPSO, LTD.
There's a tea and cappuccino bar at the back of this unusual gift shop, which includes many "environmentally correct" products, and you can sample many blends while you consider what to buy. There are locally made sauces, jellies from Anegada, jewelry made in St. Thomas and St. John, Caribbean cookbooks, island music, neat children's toys, local spices, skin care products, and coffees and teas. *340-776-2303. Inside the A. H. Riise Mall; enter from western entrance on Main St. and walk straight back through the watches.*

60

CARIBBEAN PRINT GALLERY

Come here for a great selection of greeting cards, stunning books including MAPes MONDe editions, lovely Caribbean maps, and frameable Caribbean watercolors and paintings. They carry poster tubes for easy traveling. This is a popular spot and also somewhat cramped, but worth the stop, so if it's too crowded for you, just come back later in the day. *340-776-2886. On Main St., in the middle of the A. H. Riise building.*

DOWN ISLAND TRADERS

There is much more to this store than the T-shirts and Caribbean teas, coffees, spices, and jams just inside the entrance. Look for a delightful potpourri of island wares—pottery from the St. Thomas Kilnworks, hand-painted Christmas tree ornaments, island artwork, watercolor maps of the Caribbean, cards and watercolors by Flukes of the BVI, teas and coffees, greeting cards and cookbooks, beach bags, colorful beach towels, and sterling silver jewelry. And don't forget to look up. Lots of great stuff hangs from the ceiling. *340-776-4641. East end of Waterfront Hwy. shops, just west of Vendors' Plaza.*

CLOTHING (CASUAL)

CLUB RYNO

Of Myrtle Beach, Charleston, and Egg Harbor fame, Club Ryno showcases casual fashions for men and women, including Tommy Bahama dresses, shirts, shorts, and pants. You'll also find sandals and shoes, hats, purses, and belts. On the east side of the alley is Club Ryno Accessories, with just accessories, including a great selection of DYNK sunglasses. *340-777-9670. West side of south end of Palm Passage, near the waterfront.*

INSTEP

Keep in step with island fashion in this charming shop which carries casual women's sundresses (from very short to ankle length) in neat cotton or rayon prints, interesting hats, beautiful scarves, and island jewelry. *340-774-7208. Middle of east alley of Royal Dane Mall.*

LOCAL COLOR

Artist Kerry Topper owns this store. She creates the distinctive designs for her line of Local Color T-Shirts: island scenes in bright primary colors—reds, yellows, blues—framed in a big square. Terry sells her work up and down the Caribbean. You can also buy prints of her art that you can hang on the wall. This is also a good place to come for comfortable Jams dresses and shirts and a great selection of hats. There are plenty of clothes for kids here, too. *340-774-3727. Halfway down Hibiscus Alley, just west of A. H. Riise Walkway.*

PUSSER'S COMPANY STORE

If you haven't yet experienced one of the very popular Pusser's Company stores, now is your chance. They are found all over the British Virgin Islands and are one of the best places to shop for comfortable Pusser's sportswear for the whole family. You'll also find a good assortment of island books, appealing souvenirs, and, naturally, the famous Pusser's Rum, available in interesting decanters as well as standard bottles. *340-777-9281. On A. H. Riise Walkway, four alleys west of the Post Office.*

CLOTHING (DESIGNER)

COSMOPOLITAN

Come here for Gottex, Bally, Paul & Shark, and Burma Bibas labels. There's a great selection of women's swimwear and swimwear cover-ups. There's also swimwear for men and tennis wear for men and women plus men's slacks, shirts, shorts, and accessories—including belts and ties. Be sure to check out the upstairs also. *340-776-2040. Waterfront Hwy. at Drake's Passage.*

DKNY

The inviting interior of this shop is sleek and spare, a perfect background for the very sophisticated DKNY clothing. Drop in here to pick up some of the latest and trendiest DKNY designs, including suits, jackets, silk sweaters, blouses, pants, jeans, silk scarves, and belts. *340-774-1688. Midway into Palm Passage.*

JANINE'S BOUTIQUE

Stop here for an excellent and ever-changing collection of designer fashion clothing and upscale accessories for women and for men. You'll find selections from Louis Ferand, Cacheral, Christian Dior, Pierre Cardin, YSL, and Valentino. *340-774-8243. Midway into Palm Passage.*

NICOLE MILLER BOUTIQUE

Nicole Miller became famous for her absolutely stunning, delightfully whimsical ties and now, of course, she fashions all manner of things out of these amusing silk prints. They're all available here—umbrellas, dop kits, address books, boxer shorts, swim suits, bathrobes, vests, jackets. Come here for a huge selection of her wildly popular and ever-changing collection of ties. Stop here also for Ms. Miller's line of very sexy and feminine dresses—in solids as well as her famous prints. The 1300-square-foot boutique with white marble floor and white stucco arches is a cool classy interior to show off Ms. Miller's sensational silk designs. The courteous staff will help you find what you want. *340-774-8286. On Main St. at Palm Passage.*

SOFT TOUCH BOUTIQUE

Shop here for a great selection of classy silk dresses, linen dresses, dressy beaded gowns, silk shirts and blouses, and pants. There are lots of designer labels and also many, many selections in petite sizes. Prices are quite good. *340-776-1760. In Grand Hotel complex, east of the Post Office.*

TESTANI UOMO

Beautifully made Italian designer clothing for men is on display at this elegant store. Check out the silk shirts, cashmere sweaters, silk and linen slacks, and elegant ties. It's a bargain compared to prices in Italy, but still quite expensive. *340-714-2470. North side of Grand Hotel complex.*

TOMMY HILFIGER

Those of you who can't get enough Tommy Hilfiger items will want to head into this huge store, which has a bit of everything you can imagine, all branded with his famous moniker. *340-777-1189. Waterfront at Royal Dane Mall.*

CHOCOLATES AND OTHER GREAT CANDIES
A CHEW OR TWO

This is a chocoholic's super-heaven. You might want to just sniff and savor the Godiva chocolate in the air before getting down to deciding exactly which Godiva truffle you should sample first. It's okay (if you can do it) to go in and just have one. In fact people do this again and again, all day long. If you're stuck, Donna Hodge from Tortola can help you choose from tray after tray of tempting truffles—double chocolate raspberry truffles, chocolate truffles with Moet & Chandon Champagne or Cognac or Amaretto, French Vanilla truffles with Myers's Rum, or Black Cherry truffles. There are also rum balls, rum cakes, sugar-free chocolates, West Indian jellies, Godiva coffees (hot and by the cup as well as packaged), and gourmet jelly beans (the pear ones are particularly awesome) which you can buy by individual flavor or choose your own mix. *340-774-6675. On Trompeter Gade, one alley east of the Royal Dane Mall complex.*

CIGARS
RIO CIGARS

When you want the finest smoke around, step into this blond wood and glass shop and check out your pleasure. Cigar aficionados sometimes spend hours in the large walk-in humidor here, swooning over the vast selection of handmade stogies. There's a full bar here, too, in case you want to try one of your purchases with a glass of aged malt or a martini. *340-774-5877. Behind Java Wraps in the Royal Dane Mall.*

DRUGSTORE
ST. THOMAS APOTHECARY
If you've run out of your favorite shampoo, shaving cream, or deodorant, or need bandaids or cotton balls, or want a prescription filled, just walk right through Mr. Tablecloth and up several steps. You'll be in a full-service drugstore complete with magazines, candies, hairdryers, cosmetics, heating pads, pain relievers, and even a full-time pharmacist. You can drop off your prescription from the states before you shop and pick it up in an hour or two and you can even have your stateside doctor phone in a prescription. *340-774-5432. Corner of Main St. and Nye Gade.*

GIFTS AND UNUSUAL ITEMS
DEL SOL
Stuff may look a bit dull inside this shop but take anything here into the sun and then watch out! Like magic, black and white or blue and white designs on T-shirts, beach bags, beach towels, swim trunks, and more transform into a riot of color! And there's more. Nail polish switches from one vivid shade to another. Sunglasses completely change shades. Markers (the kind you draw with) go from one color to another. It's so cool! *340-774-2753. Waterfront at Royal Dane Mall.*

SHIPWRECKERS ANTIQUES
The unassuming entrance here leads to a delightful surprise. It's a wonderful store to wander about in. The owner also owns a salvage shop which is how he found much of what you see here. The exposed brick walls are hung with artwork and old maps of the Caribbean, brilliantly colored live parrots speak their mind, and antique parts of boats are on display (and also for sale). There are beautiful ship wheels and lanterns, plus old coins, maps, and books on the Caribbean. There are even old USVI license plates. *340-774-2074. On the most western Royal Dane Mall alley.*

TRITON'S TRUMPET
Come to this terrific shop for a simply grand selection of 100% cotton pillow covers and bedspreads hand-painted with wonderful, colorful designs. Handsome baskets, beds, hand-carved wooden cabinets, graceful vases, comfortable pareos, African masks, scatter rugs, soft throws, charming wooden boxes, and so much more are artfully arranged in this spacious store with a mix of deep pastel and lovely stone walls. Items here are from around the world and there's a lot to see. Be sure to look for the interesting stamps that are used to create the hand-painted patterns. They are for sale, too. *340-774-4252. Middle of east alley of Royal Dane Mall.*

JEWELRY AND SCULPTURES
BERNARD K. PASSMAN GALLERY

This is a remarkable store and gallery showcasing exquisite pieces of jewelry and delicate small black coral sculptures by world-famous Bernard Passman: a miniature piano with all 88 keys and delicate gold pedals ($22,000); a miniature drum set complete with cymbals and several miniature drums—look for the swirls on the drums, which are the natural swirls in the coral ($28,000), a delicate image of a can-can girl with 22 karat gold boots ($175,000). Perhaps the most famous sculpture is that of Charlie Chaplin, with his dog—in solid gold—next to him. It's been valued at $1.2 million. So, what can a regular person afford? Beautiful gold and black coral bracelets, striking diamond and black coral rings, and lovely pendants in the shape of fish with gold eyes. Prices start at $60 and every single piece is exquisitely detailed and initialed. The sales people treat the place as an art gallery and are very warm and friendly and will happily explain the interesting histories behind the more famous pieces even if you are just a browser. *340-777-4580. On Main St., one block west of the Post Office.*

OKIDANOKH GOLDCRAFT

Arched doorways, brick walls, and fanciful illustrations of unicorns and hot air balloons create a peaceful setting for display tables showcasing finely handcrafted gold and silver jewelry. Come here for delicate and highly original earrings, necklaces, bracelets, and pendants. *340-774-9677. Back of Royal Dane Mall.*

LEATHER PURSES & LUGGAGE
LEATHER SHOP

Step in here, take a deep breath, and savor the smell of expensive leather. This place has a great selection of classy imported handbags, wallets, purses, briefcases, and luggage. Prices are a lot lower than stateside. Check out the sale shelves—usually past the sales counter on the left. There can be truly exceptional bargains here (and at the Havensight branch also). *340-776-0290. Main St., a block west of the Post Office. "Fendi" is on the door.*

OCEAN LEATHER

You'll be astonished to discover that all the fine leather goods on display— wallets, photo albums, purses, business card cases, organizers in all manner of colors—are crafted out of fish skin, mostly from Pacific salmon. Not only is it soft and supple, it wears extremely well, it's not expensive, and it is environmentally friendly (the skins are by-products of fish farms). *340-714-2880. Back in east end of Royal Dane Mall.*

PURSES AND THINGS

Walls and tables here are chock full of luggage, change purses, briefcases, handbags, satchels, checkbook wallets, billfolds, and passport cases in all sizes and styles and all made of soft and supple Columbian leather. Everything feels so good here that you'll want it all and prices are very reasonable. There are also good choices of colors. *340-777-9717. Near Chase bank in International Plaza Alley.*

LINGERIE
LOVER'S LANE

Follow the narrow stairs up to this hedonistic den of lingerie and bedtime pleasures. Pick out some sexy underwear, or exotic swimwear, or find a romantic gift. The more adventurous will be interested in the various items displayed along the walls. *340-777-9616. Waterfront between Raadet's Gade and Hibiscus Alley.*

SHOES AND SANDALS
SHOE TREE

This is an excellent spot for brand name ladies' shoes. You'll find a good selection of sandals, comfortable flats, and dressy heels. Check out the sale shoes on the floor by the cash register. There's almost always at least one great bargain. *340-774-3900. On Cardow's Walk, just beyond the entrance to Bumpa's Cafe.*

ZORA'S

Zora's has been here since 1962 and people come from all over the world for custom-made leather sandals that are exquisitely comfortable and last close to forever. There are also ready-made sandals, canvas bags, famous limin' shoes, Great Wall of China backpacks, kids' canvas shark and fish purses, belly bags, and monster backpacks that look, well, just like monsters. If you want custom-made sandals, it takes five days so head here on your first or second day of vacation to get measured and to chose a style (there are at least 50, named after nifty places on nearby islands, like Joe's Hill on Tortola). Before you head home you can stop in for a final fitting and to get your sandals. Zora, her daughter, and Ann are caring craftspeople. Be sure to take one of their catalogues home with you. That way, when you get home and wish you'd bought that neat cat bag, or want to order another pair of limin' shoes, or decide you want to do all your Christmas shopping at Zora's, you can! *340-774-2559. From the Post Office walk east on Main St. Go over the little hill and look for the stoplight in the distance. The store is on the right, just before the stoplight, where you see a balcony.*

SWIM AND BEACH WEAR

GOING SEANILE

It beats getting old! If you can use it near water, you'll probably find what you need in this little shop for sunning and beach needs, from sunglasses to sandals, reef shoes, visor hats, bathing suits, swim trunks, and T-shirts, many showing off their wacky logo. *340-774-1510. Waterfront at Royal Dane Mall.*

JUST ADD WATER TOO

Racks here are filled with the hottest new swimsuit designs. There are teeny bikinis, flattering two-piece suits, and one-piece suits cut slim and full. If you need a cover-up, you can find one here also. *340-776-7946. Middle of Royal Dane Mall.*

TAPES AND CDs

PARROT FISH

This is a good spot to choose if you want to sample some Caribbean music. You'll find reggae, steel drum, fungi and more plus top-40 and other music from the U.S. *340-776-4514. Back St. at Stortvaer Gade.*

SAM GOODY

For the hottest and latest tapes and compact discs and for swing, alternative music, soft and hard rock, easy listening, classical music, oldies—whatever you seek, you'll probably find it in this large upstairs store. There are videos, too. *340-774-8092. Above the Leather Shop on Main St.*

VISITORS' HOSPITALITY LOUNGE

VISITORS' HOSPITALITY LOUNGE

Many visitors don't know that there is a wonderful hospitality lounge run by volunteers that is just for you! Stop here and rest your feet or use the restroom. Settle into a chair and browse through brochures on what to do and where to go. Buy a book (they have several books for sale, including some neat children's books) or buy a soda or a bottle of icy cold water. If you are on your way to or from the airport, you can even leave your luggage here! There's a small charge per piece, according to size. And please leave a donation. *340-777-8827. Right in the Grand Hotel complex across from Emancipation Park.*

FOR A MAP
SHOWING THE LOCATION
OF SHOPS DESCRIBED HERE,
JUST TURN THE PAGE.

67

SHOPS IN CHARLOTTE AMALIE
SEE MAP FOR LOCATION

ANTIQUES
Carson Co. Antiques-26
BOOKS, NEWSPAPERS
Island Newsstand-4
CARIBBEAN ITEMS
Calypso-12
Caribbean Print Gallery-11
Down Island Traders-6
CLOTHING (CASUAL)
Club Ryno-32
Instep-19
Local Color-14
Pusser's Company Store-13
CLOTHING (DESIGNER)
Cosmopolitan-16
DKNY-31
Janine's Boutique-30
Nicole Miller-29
Soft Touch Boutique-3
Testani Uomo-2
Tommy Hilfiger-22
CHOCOLATES & CANDIES
A Chew or Two-17
CIGARS
Rio Cigars-21
DRUGSTORE
St. Thomas Apothecary-35

GIFTS & UNUSUAL ITEMS
Del Sol-25
Shipwreckers-27
Triton's Trumpet-18
JEWELRY
Bernard K. Passman Gallery-9
Okidanokh Goldcraft-23
LEATHER
Leather Shop-7
Ocean Leather-20
Purses and Things-33
LINGERIE
Lover's Lane-15
SHOES & SANDALS
Shoe Tree-10
Zora's-1
SWIM AND BEACH WEAR
Cosmopolitan-16
Going Seanile-28
Just Add Water Too-24
TAPES & CDS
Parrot Fish-34
Sam Goody-8
VISITORS'
HOSPITALITY LOUNGE-5

1. Zora's
2. Testani Uomo
3. Soft Touch Boutique
4. Island Newsstand
5. Visitors' Lounge
6. Down Island Traders
7. Leather Shop
8. Sam Goody
9. Bernard K. Passman
10. Shoe Tree
11. Caribbean Print Gallery
12. Calypso
13. Pusser's
14. Local Color
15. Lover's Lane
16. Cosmopolitan
17. A Chew or Two
18. Triton's Trumpet
19. Instep
20. Ocean Leather
21. Rio Cigars
22. Tommy Hilfiger
23. Okidanokh Goldcraft
24. Just Add Water Too
25. Del Sol
26. Carson Co. Antiques
27. Shipwreckers
28. Going Seanile
29. Nicole Miller
30. Janine's Boutique
31. DKNY
32. Club Ryno
33. Purses and Things
34. Parrot Fish
35. St. Thomas Apothecary

CHARLOTTE AMALIE SHOP LOCATIONS

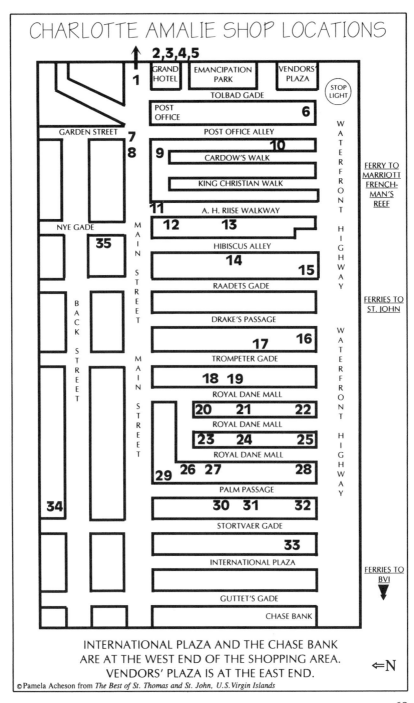

INTERNATIONAL PLAZA AND THE CHASE BANK
ARE AT THE WEST END OF THE SHOPPING AREA.
VENDORS' PLAZA IS AT THE EAST END.

⇐N

© Pamela Acheson from *The Best of St. Thomas and St. John, U.S. Virgin Islands*

HAVENSIGHT SHOPPING

Havensight was built to make it easy for cruise ship passengers to shop without having to go anywhere. Original shops and small branches of many of the duty-free Charlotte Amalie stores are located here in four long one-story buildings that stretch back from the cruise ship dock. Also here is the red-roofed Ports of Sale complex. Havensight is never really that crowded and this is an easy place to check out duty-free bargains whether or not you are on a cruise ship and if you don't want to go to town.

DOCKSIDE BOOKSHOP

For a superb selection of books in the best bookstore in the Virgin Islands, head straight here. You'll find two floors loaded with hard- and soft-cover best sellers, shelves and shelves of novels, mysteries, and adventures, plus books on travel, hobbies, cookbooks, and more. Check out the shelf to the right of the cash register for wonderful books on St. Thomas, the Virgin Islands, and the whole Caribbean. *340-774-4937. Havensight Mall.*

MODERN MUSIC

Across the street from Havensight is this great tape and CD store. Come here for the latest stateside releases plus loads of island music, including albums by Bankie Banx, a terrific recording star from Anguilla. *340-774-3100. Across the street from Havensight's main entrance.*

ST. THOMAS' BEST MARKET

MARINA MARKET IN RED HOOK

This is absolutely the best market on St. Thomas. Come here for really fresh produce—red and yellow peppers, portobello mushrooms, yellow tomatoes, numerous lettuces; for excellent wines and champagnes; for specialty items; for a great assortment of upscale stateside brand grocery items; and for a truly great butcher—place your custom order or choose marinated chicken breasts, small rack of lamb, whole tenderloins, or ground sirloin. Come here also for excellently prepared food to go—home-made mashed potatoes, grilled chicken, and a great salad bar. Take it home or eat outside on the little terrace. *340-779-2411.*

RED HOOK SHOPPING

For years, if you were staying on the east end of St. Thomas, you had to "make do" with Red Hook. Yes, you could buy necessities (there was a grocery store and a pharmacy and a gas station), but it was mainly where visitors went to hop a ferry to St. John or to the British Virgin Islands. Now you will find that there are several quite delightful one-of-a-kind shops.

CHRIS SAWYER DIVING STORE
In addition to diving gear, there are bathing suits, sunglasses, hats, sandals, snorkel gear, and a good selection of postcards. *340-777-7804. Downtown Red Hook.*

ELIZABETH JAMES
In this appealing jewelry and clothing boutique, quality rather than quantity is the name of the game. There isn't a lot of any one thing but everything here is truly special and nicely displayed. At the back of the store are beaded dresses, washable silk scoop tops, crepe evening slacks, and linen and silk blouses. The front of the store is the showcase for sterling silver and 14k jewelry, much of which is hand made. This is also the only place besides St. Croix where you can buy the famous Crucian Hook Bracelet that is made in St. Croix. She also carries Crucian Hook earrings and rings. *340-779-1595. Downtown Red Hook.*

THE COLOR OF JOY
Shelves and racks are crowded and aisles are narrow, so take your time here because there is lots of great stuff. It ranges from clothing to gift items to terrific local artwork. Look for light and loose and very pretty cotton dresses and sundresses, colorful hand-painted scarves, great sandals, comfortable sarongs, little sculptures, locally crafted ceramics, and an intriguing selection of local art. *340-775-4020. Downtown Red Hook.*

RHIANNON'S
Glittery and magical fairy dust that you can scatter about for good luck is just one of the delightful things you will find in this New Age store. Stunning quilts by local artists hang on the walls. Tables display spell boxes, good quality incense sticks, a huge array of candles, wonderful books of all sizes, and so much more. There are also delicate earrings, bracelets, and necklaces. If you'd like a tarot reading, just make an appointment. *340-779-1877. Downtown Red Hook.*

71

GREAT ST. THOMAS SHOPPING FINDS

Cruzan Sterling Silver Bracelets
Godiva Chocolate Truffles
Custom Leather Sandals
The New York Times
Old Virgin Island License Plates
Local Spices and Jams
Leather Luggage
Reggae CDs
Nicole Miller Ties
T-shirts from Local Color
Pusser's Rum & Pusser's Sportswear
Gauzy Dresses
MAPes MONDe Books & Old Maps

GREAT THINGS TO LOOK FOR

THE BIRDS YOU WERE FEEDING LAST SUMMER

Don't be surprised if some of the birds you see look a lot like the songbirds you had in your backyard last summer. They head here from North America every winter, too. Some actually go all the way to South America, stopping here on the way down and on the way back north.

HITCH-HIKING BIRDS

If you take a ferry anywhere, look to see if a bird seems to "hang in the air" close to the boat. It'll be a Brown Booby, hitching a ride. You'll see them actually search out a power boat so they can catch a ride in the boat's air wake. If they spot a fish, they'll swoop right down and catch it and then race like crazy to catch back up to the boat to continue their "extra-easy" ride.

HOMEMADE FREIGHTERS

Head down to the Charlotte Amalie waterfront and walk along the harbor until you see some small cargo boats. Stop and read the handmade signs in front of some of the vessels: "Will take cargo to Dominica, Guadaloupe, and St. Lucia" or "Leaving for Sint Maarten tonight." These small boats travel from island to island, often carrying bananas or other produce north to St. Thomas and bringing much-needed freight back to some of the southern Caribbean islands.

LOCAL KNOWLEDGE

PERFUME DEALS
You can get great deals on cosmetics and perfumes not only while you are on St. Thomas, but even after you return home. Simply call the Perfume Palace at 800-289-8784 and place your order.

RECYCLED BALLAST
Many of the bricks used in the buildings on St. Thomas were originally used simply as ballast on the ships that came to St. Thomas to pick up cargo. These ships dumped the bricks and filled their hulls with rum and sugar and returned to Europe.

GETTING LOST
Don't feel stupid if you can't find the store you were in five minutes ago when you are shopping in Charlotte Amalie. This happens to everyone—including people who have lived on St. Thomas for years.

OPENING DAYS
Some restaurants are closed on Sundays . . . several on Mondays, and a few on Tuesdays. But also the days may change at different times of the year. It's probably best to call first on these days or nights.

DOMINOS
You can play dominos or whist every Wednesday and Saturday night at Percy's Bus Stop. If you're interested, call Percy at 340-774-5993.

CHAPTER 5

GREAT CHARLOTTE AMALIE LUNCH BREAKS

"Ask not what you can do for your country.
Ask what's for lunch."

—*Orson Welles*

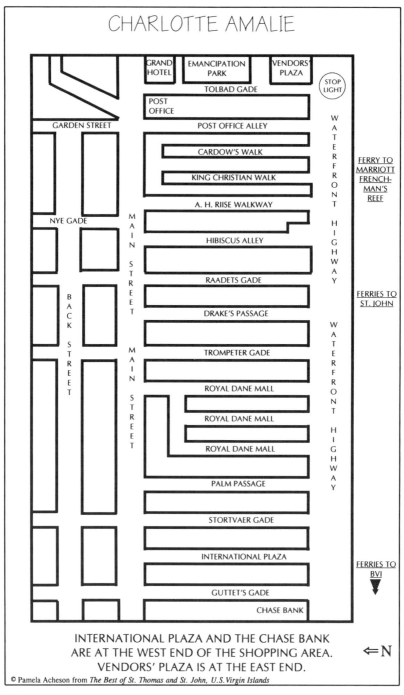

CHARLOTTE AMALIE

INTERNATIONAL PLAZA AND THE CHASE BANK
ARE AT THE WEST END OF THE SHOPPING AREA. ⇐N
VENDORS' PLAZA IS AT THE EAST END.

© Pamela Acheson from *The Best of St. Thomas and St. John, U.S. Virgin Islands*

GREAT CHARLOTTE AMALIE LUNCH BREAKS

There are many places along the waterfront or tucked in alleyways in between shops where you can pause and have breakfast or lunch or a snack or just a cool beverage. These spots are generally open from about 7:30 a.m. to 4 or 5 p.m., although some stay open later in season. Those that don't serve breakfast open around 11 a.m. Directions at the end of each description correlate to the map at left.

BOBBY'S

Tables are close together and it can often look too crowded at Bobby's but once you're seated, it's okay. Stop by for good Caesar salad with grilled chicken, taco salad, hamburgers, pizza, barbecued pork tenderloin sandwich, and their homemade veggie burger. *340-774-6054. Entrances on both Trompeter Gade and Drake's Passage.*

BUMPA'S

This outdoor, second floor cafe is a place to escape the hustle and bustle below. Gaze out at the harbor while you sip coffee and munch on a blueberry muffin or bacon and eggs. Hamburgers and sandwiches are on the lunch menu and the ice cream is great. They turn the grill off at 4:00 p.m. but you can get sandwiches until 5:00 p.m. The puzzle is how do you get up to Bumpa's since there is no visible entrance on Waterfront Highway. Steps are just around the west corner. *340-776-5674. Waterfront Hwy. at Cardow's Walk.*

CAFE AMICI

This stop in Riise's Alley offers a peaceful oasis away from the traffic. Umbrellas shade the little marble-top tables which are set on a long, narrow brick terrace. There's always a soup, quiche, pasta, and sandwich of the day and the menu includes sandwiches, salads, and pastas. The stuffed mushrooms, penne pesto, and grilled eggplant sandwich are delicious. Breads are baked fresh daily and irresistible. Teas and appetizers are offered in the afternoon. *340-776-5670. A.H. Riise Walkway.*

CLUB RYNO TROPICAL CAFE

Belly up to the long outdoor bar or find a seat under an umbrella at one of the round tables scattered about Palm Passage and dine on a crisp Caesar salad or a juicy cheeseburger or sample the fresh catch of the day. *Closed Sun. 340-777-8015. Palm Passage.*

GLADYS' CAFE

Gladys has owned several restaurants since she moved here from Antigua in 1969 and locals seek out her West Indian specialties, such as chicken soup with pigeon peas, pan-fried yellow tail with Creole sauce, curried chicken, and lemon-buttered conch. But she also prepares excellent hamburgers, salads, and meatloaf with mashed potatoes. Tired shoppers like to relax with one of Gladys' special soursop coladas. *340-774-6604. Royal Dane Mall.*

GREEN HOUSE

This popular Waterfront Highway place is open to the breezes and busy all day long (and actually well into the evening). Come here for a late breakfast (they open at 10:30 a.m.) of huevos rancheros or eggs Benedict or a Creole omelet. Hamburgers, cheeseburgers, hot dogs, salads, a variety of sandwiches, and pizzas are served at lunch. *340-774-7998. Waterfront, west of Palm Passage at Stortvaer Gade, near Chase bank.*

HARD ROCK CAFE

Booths and tables sit among rock 'n' roll decor at this typically-decorated Hard Rock Cafe. The moderate-priced menu features chili, cheese nachos, chef salad, California club (a BLT with a grilled marinated chicken breast and Swiss cheese), and their incredibly popular "Pig Sandwich" plus hamburgers and cheeseburgers, sundaes, banana splits, shakes and malts, and root beer floats. *No breakfast but open well into the evening. 340-777-5555. Waterfront at International Plaza.*

HERVE

If you want a sophisticated setting, the comfort of air-conditioning, and a superb view of the harbor, walk up past the park across from the Post Office and then follow the stairs up to this excellent restaurant. The lunch menu features corn fritters, escargot, a delicious onion soup, many salads (including Caesar, chef, and roast duck), seafood crepes, quiche of the day, a tasty croque monsieur, and burgers. *No lunch Sat.-Sun. 340-777-9703. Government Hill.*

SO SOUP ME

If you like homemade soups and pastries, definitely head here. You can eat in or take out. The soups change daily but there are always many choices, such as red pea with pork, clam chowder, chicken noodle, seafood kallaloo, and Cuban black bean. Freshly-baked pastries are also a specialty at this little shop. Don't miss the cherry danish and don't leave without a chocolate chip cookie or two. You can get good sandwiches here, also. *340-777-5366. Back St. at Stortvaer Gade.*

TAVERN ON THE WATERFRONT

Tables line the windows at this indoor, upstairs eatery overlooking the harbor. The eclectic menu is globally inspired, and presentations are beautiful, whether you opt for an over-stuffed sandwich, a fresh salad, or the superb crab tempura. *340-776-4328. Waterfront Hwy. at Royal Dane Mall.*

WEST INDIES' COFFEE

It's easy to miss this one. The entrance is less than entrancing and you can't tell until you've walked a few steps inside that this is actually a wonderful cappuccino and espresso bar. Daily specials are on the blackboard and there are numerous baked goods. *340-774-9763. Hibiscus Alley.*

VIRGILIO'S

When you want an elegant lunch and some of the best Italian food anywhere, come here. Soft lighting and polished service provide the perfect backdrop for a glass of champagne, a salad, and freshly grilled fish or the pasta of the day. Although Virgin Island power lunches are held here, Virgilio's is really meant for lingering and it's a fine place for a long and leisurely lunch. *Reservations are a good idea. 340-776-4920. Main St. at Stortvaer Gade.*

SNACKS AND ICE CREAM
ICE CREAM SHOPPE

This tiny take-away place has delicious ice cream cones, yogurt, and hot dogs, plus West Indian snacks like fish fry, johnnie cakes, chicken soup, and meat pates. *Tucked next to the Hard Rock Cafe souvenir store.*

ZELDA'S STAND

When you're ready for a bottle of ice-cold water or a cold, cold soda, head to this little stand. There's no sign so look for a pretty lady who's wearing a colorful wide-brimmed bonnet and a beautiful smile. Her stand is simply a little silver cart and a cooler but she's got icy cold sodas, bottled water, and juices, plus candy, sugar cakes, chips, and little bags of peanuts. And she can see the good side of just about everything. *Tolbad Gade, between the Post Office and Waterfront Hwy, across from Vendor's Plaza.*

79

THE CHILI COOKOFF

If you like chili and happen to be in St. Thomas in late summer or early fall, check with the Texas Society of the Virgin Islands and see if you're lucky enough to be on island during their annual Chili Cookoff. It's one of the island's great happenings!

Several thousand people show up for this all-day event. The Chili Judges (chili connoisseurs, naturally) rate chili samples for aroma, color, and consistency and take into consideration both the immediate taste and the equally important aftertaste.

Once the judges have had their fill, the general public is welcome to sample as many chili offerings as they can, for a quarter each.

The Chili Cookoff is held on a beach (which one varies year to year). There's live music all day long, and there are all kinds of games and contests—tug-o-war and melon seed spitting, to name just two—and a bunch of prizes. It's a great event and a lot of fun and money raised goes to local charities.

ST. JOHN FOR THE EVENING

Many visitors to St. Thomas never realize how incredibly easy it is to head over to St. John just for dinner. In fact, if you are staying on the east end of St. Thomas, it is possible to go to St. John for dinner in about the same length of time that it would take you to get to downtown Charlotte Amalie.

Most of the ferries have an uncovered upper level and you can ride over basking in the afternoon sun and return at night in a seat open to the soft Caribbean breezes and under a blanket of stars and perhaps a full moon.

Getting there on a ferry.
The ferry dock is right in the middle of the east end of St. Thomas, at Red Hook. Ferries run hourly from Red Hook to Cruz Bay on St. John and the ride takes less than 20 minutes. Get there a little early if you want to be sure to get a seat up top. The fare is $3 and the ferry takes you to the dock right in the heart of Cruz Bay, which is St. John's only real town and very different from anything on St. Thomas. If you prefer a private ride, **Dohm Water Taxi** (*340-775-6501*) will take you over to St. John in one of their power catamarans in a quick 15 minutes and bring you back after dinner. It's $15 per person (minimum of five people) each way.

Note: Ferries leave Cruz Bay on the hour until 11 p.m. If you miss this one, well...you're on St. John for the night.

81

A
FULL DAY
IN PARADISE

A breakfast in bed or on a beach
A morning stroll and a swim
A few pages under the palms
maybe a massage
A junket to St. John with lunch in
Cruz Bay
A dessert or two by the dock
A soft drink for the voyage back
Another swim, a nap, a bubble bath
A cocktail under the stars
A romantic repast for two
A barefoot dance in the breezes
A port on the porch. . . and
then to bed.

CHAPTER 6

GREAT
ST. THOMAS
BEACHES
&
WATERSPORTS

"Babies don't need a vacation, but
I still see them at the beach."
—*Steven Wright*

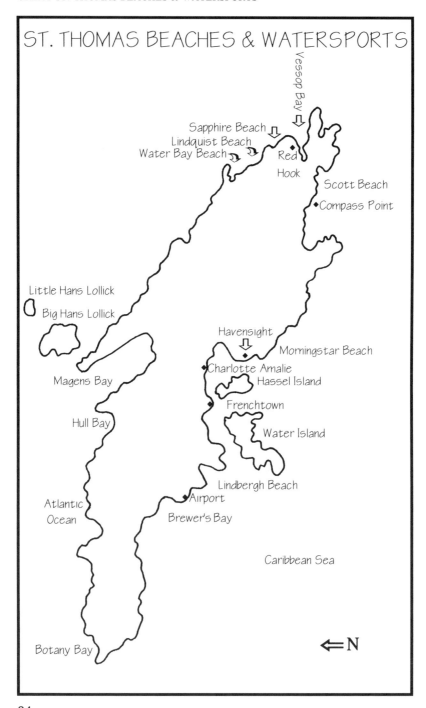

ST. THOMAS BEACHES & WATERSPORTS

Vessop Bay

Sapphire Beach
Lindquist Beach
Water Bay Beach
Red Hook
Scott Beach
Compass Point

Little Hans Lollick
Big Hans Lollick

Havensight
Morningstar Beach
Charlotte Amalie
Magens Bay
Hassel Island
Frenchtown
Hull Bay
Water Island

Lindbergh Beach
Airport
Atlantic Ocean
Brewer's Bay

Caribbean Sea

Botany Bay

⇐N

GREAT BEACHES

St. Thomas has many great beaches. Some are undeveloped. Others are in front of resorts. On St. Thomas, as in all of the USVI, all beaches are open to everyone, even if there's a resort there. Bear in mind that a beach in front of a resort is "groomed" at least once or twice a day. Workers pick up trash, rake the sand, and clip and water the tropical foliage that borders the beach. Anyone used to a "groomed" beach can think a natural beach in the Caribbean looks "messy," but it's not really. It's just that there's no one around to remove the seaweed, or pick up the detritus the waves have tossed on shore.

BOTANY BAY BEACH
It's way out at the western tip of the island, a very long drive and a bit of a walk, but the snorkeling is quite good here.

BREWER'S BAY BEACH
This beach is west of the airport (keep the airport on the left as you drive west on Brewer's Bay Drive—Rte 30, and then drive all the way through the campus of the University of the Virgin Islands.) This is a nice swimming beach and there are several snack trucks on weekends. This beach is close to the final approach to the St. Thomas airport and is a great place to see planes of all sizes.

HULL BAY BEACH
You'll see lots of little painted fishing boats bouncing at their buoys at this north shore beach. It's not a great swimming beach because there are so many little boats and it can be rough when the surf is up. Larry's Hideaway Bar and Grill, a bit behind the beach, is a popular barefoot bar with weekend entertainment. The menu ranges from hot dogs to sandwiches to linguini with meat sauce.

LINDBERGH BEACH
Practically across the street from the airport, this nice long beach is great for walking and is also a calm swimming beach. Not very many large planes fly in and out of St. Thomas so the airport noise really isn't a problem. There are several hotels here, including the Island Beachcomber. You can rent jet skis and waverunners and go waterskiing here. There's also some fine food to be had at the little snack bar wagons parked along the road.

LINDQUIST BEACH
Also called Smith Bay Beach, it's on the eastern shore and it's one of the few easily-accessible beaches that is still completely undeveloped (although plans

85

threaten to change this). The swimming here is excellent. This is a nice long beach lined with sea grapes. It's great for walking and taking in the views of Thatch Cay and Grass Cay. From Smith Bay Road (between the entrance to Pavilions and Pools and the Wyndham Sugar Bay) two dirt roads just yards from each other lead to this beach. One is about a minute north of Pavilions and Pools, is quite bumpy, and can involve encounters with big cows. The less bumpy, easier (no cows) dirt road is just a few yards further on and two signs make it easy to spot—coming from Red Hook, look for the green airport sign. If you're heading to Red Hook, turn left at the 35 mph sign.

MAGENS BAY BEACH
Year after year this long and stunning north shore beach is voted one of the world's ten most beautiful beaches, and unfortunately it's both popular and easy to reach. It was donated to St. Thomas by Arthur S. Fairchild in 1946 (along with 45 adjoining acres) to be preserved forever as a public park. The beach is a very long gentle curve of dazzling white sand and the water is exceptionally calm. There's $1 per vehicle and $1 per person entrance fee and you can rent beach chairs, floats, towels, snorkeling equipment, and lockers. There's a cafeteria-style snack bar and a large beachwear shop.

MORNINGSTAR BEACH
Just outside of St. Thomas harbor, this beach is at Marriott's Frenchman's Reef and Morning Star Resorts and there are several restaurants and bars along the beach. You can rent beach chairs, snorkel and windsurfing equipment, and take windsurfing and sunfish lessons. The beach is fairly long and generally calm for swimming, although it can have a little swell.

SAPPHIRE BEACH
This half-mile-long beach fronts the Sapphire Beach Resort on the east end of St. Thomas. You can parasail from here, rent waverunners and sunfish, take windsurfing and scuba diving lessons, and rent floats and beach chairs.

SCOTT BEACH
It's at the southeastern end of the island near Compass Point. You can rent beach lounges and umbrellas.

VESSUP BAY BEACH
This quiet beach is usually calm for swimming. It's near Cabrita Point.

WATER BAY BEACH
At the Renaissance Grand Beach Resort, this 1000-foot-long beach is a good spot to rent jet skis, pedal boats, windsurfers, sunfish, and waverunners.

GREAT WATERSPORTS

St. Thomas offers practically every watersport imaginable. You can snorkel off the edge of a beach, take out a sunfish, go for a sail, scuba dive day or night, try your hand at parasailing, hop onto a jet ski or a waverunner, paddle a kayak, or pedal a pedal boat. You can also rent a little powerboat or charter a boat and visit beaches on other islands. St. Thomas is also a particularly good place to try one of these activities for the first time. Watersports centers here, more so than on most islands, really do specialize in teaching the beginner as well as outfitting the expert.

JET SKIS AND WAVERUNNERS
You can skim over the waves at many locations on St. Thomas. Rent jet skis at **Marriott Frenchman's Reef Resort** (*340-776-8500*), at **Renaissance Grand Beach Resort** (*340-775-1510*), and **Caribbean Fun** (*340-715-1030*) at **Sapphire Beach Resort**.

KAYAKING
In the Virgin Islands, there are actually two kinds of kayaking. Many resorts have brightly colored one- and two-person "kayaks" which are fun to take out and you can have races or just paddle about. The kayaking sport is also popular in the Virgin Islands. You can rent real kayaks and join kayaking trips. The waters off the east end of St. Thomas have uninhabited islands and coves you can explore. Call **West Indies Wind Surfing** at Vessup Bay Beach (*340-775-6530; call first to make an appointment*). They rent kayaks and have kites that catch the wind and propel you—but don't let the wind take you too far in one direction or you'll have a long paddle back.

KAYAK/SNORKEL TRIPS
Kayak into Mangrove Lagoon with naturalists from **Virgin Island Ecotours** (*340-779-2155*) and then snorkel and see juvenile reef fish, upside down jelly fish, barracuda, and rays. There's a wonderful full moon trip that includes dinner where the phosphorescence you stir up with your paddle almost outshines the moon and the stars.

PARASAILING
Want to take a ride 500 feet above the water? This popular sport is easy to do. You don't even have to get wet. You're strapped into a parachute, a speedboat surges forward, and up you go! Boats leave from many locations. Call **Caribbean Parasailing** (*340-777-3055*).

87

PEDAL BOATS

Quite a few St. Thomas resorts have these little contraptions. They look sort of silly but once you're in one, they can be fun. Basically two people sit in a floating set of chairs and pedal around—the faster you pedal, the faster you go. It's interesting to look back at the shore and a slow trip takes almost no energy. Bring a soda or a pina colada.

POWERBOATS

On calm days it can be wonderful fun to rent your own little powerboat and tool around in the water, or find a good snorkeling spot, or explore the uninhabited islands off the east end of St. Thomas. You can take a picnic to Lavango or Mingo Cay or even head over to a beach on St. John. If it's really calm and you feel like an adventure, you can also head to the BVI (bring a passport). **Nauti Nymph** (*340-775-5066*) in Red Hook offers 25', 26', and 29' boats with bimini tops, built-in ice coolers, swim ladders, VFH radios, charts, and safety gear. **Aqua Blue** (*340-775-1242*) at Sapphire Beach rents 22' and 26' Makos with similar features. Both companies rent snorkeling gear, too.

SCUBA DIVING

St. Thomas is surrounded by lots of good diving sites. If you've always wanted to try diving, now is a good time. It's possible to take a resort course and actually dive the same day. Call **Chris Sawyer Diving Center**, with locations at Red Hook (*340-777-7804*), the Renaissance Grand Beach (*340-775-1510, ext 7850*), or the Coki Beach Dive Club (*340-775-4220*).

SNORKELING

Snorkeling equipment (mask, fins, snorkel) is available at virtually all resorts on St. Thomas and can be rented on many beaches. The water is clear here and you will see many colorful little fish. First-timers may want to try snorkeling right off the beach where it's sandy—although you won't see a lot of fish it's still interesting to look around and you can practice breathing—slow and steady is the key. Once you can breathe easily, swim over to the rocky areas and see what is going on. If you want to go on a snorkeling trip (there are many to choose from) call the **Charterboat Center** (*340-775-7990*) and they'll match you with the trip that is right for you.

WINDSURFING

Lots of people spend hours trying to stay on these things. If you don't feel like trying it yourself, do find a good spot on the beach where you can watch someone else try. It's often very funny. Most resorts rent windsurfing equipment and also give lessons. If you want to windsurf and can't at your hotel then ask at reception which would be the closest place for you to go.

GOLF & TENNIS, FITNESS CENTERS, HORSEBACK RIDING

GOLF

George and Tom Fazio designed this championship 18-hole golf course at **Mahogany Run** (*340-777-6006*) on the north side of the island. It's particularly famous for its 13th and 14th greens that sit atop a cliff high above the Atlantic.

TENNIS

Marriott's Frenchman's Reef (*340-776-8500*), **Renaissance Grand Beach Resort** (*340-775-1510*), and **Wyndham Sugar Bay** (*340-777-7100*) all have courts available for a fee to non-guests.

FITNESS CENTERS

When you feel the need for a workout, the following places have weight machines, free weights, treadmills, stairclimbers, bicycles, and even personal trainers.
Carib Health Complex at Sub Base (*340-777-1072*)
Gold's Gym (yes, just like in the states) next to the Hard Rock Cafe in Charlotte Amalie (*340-777-9474*)

HORSEBACK RIDING

See stunning vistas you just can't see from the road on an hour-long ride through trails across steep green hills and down to beaches. **Call Half Moon Stables** (*340-777-6088*) for reservations.

Some Helpful Hints

DRIVING AROUND THE ISLAND
St. Thomas is an island of spectacularly steep hills and the views up top are simply stunning. It's definitely worth it to take a drive around the island. It's nice to have the freedom of a car, but consider taking a taxi tour first—to get your bearings, to get a sense of local driving habits and the steepness of the roads, and to be able to concentrate on the scenery instead of the curves.

WHAT, NO ELECTRICITY?
Don't worry when the electricity suddenly goes off. It happens all the time and it's no big deal. (That's why you have a candle in your hotel room.) You don't even have to be very patient as the power almost always comes right back on just a few minutes later.

INVISIBLE BUGS WITH A BITE
At sundown, especially when it is not windy, annoying little 'no-see-ums' appear out of nowhere and bite. Insect repellant generally keeps them at bay and wind keeps them away. For some people, these bites have a lasting itch and it's good to have a medication like Sting-Eze around. A dab of gin will work in a pinch.

FERRY BOATS TO OTHER ISLANDS
Ferries to St. John and the British Virgin Islands leave from Red Hook and the waterfront at Charlotte Amalie. Ferries to St. Croix only leave from the Charlotte Amalie waterfront.

CHAPTER 7

GREAT
ST. THOMAS
ATTRACTIONS

"There are more than ninety-nine steps
to these ninety-nine steps."
—Peter P., age 9
from *Visiting the Virgin Islands with the Kids*

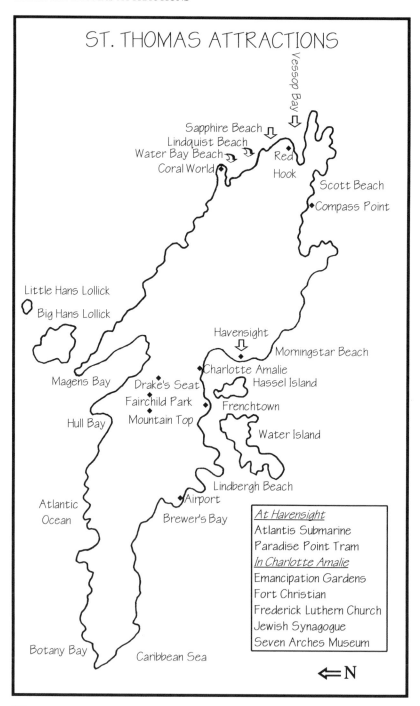

ST. THOMAS ATTRACTIONS

Vessop Bay

Sapphire Beach
Lindquist Beach
Water Bay Beach
Coral World
Red Hook

Scott Beach
Compass Point

Little Hans Lollick
Big Hans Lollick

Havensight
Morningstar Beach

Magens Bay
Drake's Seat
Charlotte Amalie
Hassel Island
Fairchild Park
Frenchtown
Hull Bay
Mountain Top

Water Island

Lindbergh Beach
Airport
Atlantic
Ocean
Brewer's Bay

At Havensight
Atlantis Submarine
Paradise Point Tram
In Charlotte Amalie
Emancipation Gardens
Fort Christian
Frederick Luthern Church
Jewish Synagogue
Seven Arches Museum

Botany Bay
Caribbean Sea

⇐N

HISTORICAL SIGHTS

There is much more to Charlotte Amalie than shopping. The town is listed in the National Register of Historic Places for its history and for its architecture. Below are descriptions of some of the most interesting buildings. If you want more information, you can find a nice selection of books and pamphlets (including an excellent walking tour) for sale in the Virgin Islands Museum shop at Fort Christian.

EMANCIPATION GARDEN
This is the park right in front of the Grand Hotel complex and is dedicated to the emancipation of the slaves in the Danish West Indies on July 3, 1848. Many local celebrations and events are held here. *Grand Hotel complex.*

FORT CHRISTIAN
You'll spot this red brick National Historic Landmark the first time you come to town. They've been restoring it for what seems like forever and there's still more to do. However, some good exhibits are open. It's the earliest known building in town and construction probably started around 1666. You can learn about famous local people, see examples of furniture that was typically in homes here 100 years ago, check out exhibits of shells, local fauna and flora, and birds. Changing exhibits by local school children focus on such things as protecting the environment and being kind to animals. There's a small room devoted to Arona Peterson's remarkable drawings of medicinal plants. *Donations welcome. 340-776-4566. Waterfront Hwy. Entrance around back.*

FREDERICK EVANGELICAL LUTHERAN CHURCH
This lovely church was established here in 1666 and the present building was started in 1789. A wide yellow brick stairway leads up to the arched entranceway. The ceiling of the church is dramatically arched and the wood in the chancel and pulpit is local mahogany. *Free. On Main Street, two blocks east of the Post Office.*

JEWISH SYNAGOGUE
Founded in 1796, this is the oldest Hebrew house of worship in continuous use under the U.S. flag. The benches and ark are fashioned out of local mahogany. The floor is sand, symbolic of a time when Jews in Spain were forced to practice their religion in secrecy and did so in cellars, using sand to muffle the sound. The walls here are made of bricks held together by sand, limestone, and molasses and it is said that years earlier children used to lick the walls to get a taste of the sweet molasses. *Donations accepted. Crystal Gade.*

93

SEVEN ARCHES MUSEUM

Ring the bell at the imposing black iron gate and someone will let you in to this restored private house, built with yellow ballast bricks from Denmark. Take a look at the stone oven in the original Danish kitchen. This is what people used to cook everything in, from stews and roasts to loaves of bread. Kids of all ages will like climbing up the steps to the high porch and seeing the many iguanas roaming about. *Small donation requested. Follow Main St. up over the hill east past the Government House and look for a little sign on the left. Follow the sign halfway down the alley.*

ATTRACTIONS AROUND THE ISLAND

St. Thomas has quite a number of "tourist attractions" but some of them really are quite special. Mountain Top and Drake's Seat are popular stops on the cruise ship crowd circuit, but you can see them without the throngs if you head to these sites in the early morning or late afternoon. Early, early morning is a great time to catch the views and take stunning photographs at scenic places that are always open, like Drake's Seat.

CORAL WORLD

The advertising can make this cluster of white geodesic domes look too "touristy" but what you see here is great and definitely worth a trip. So, what do you see? First of all, the **Underwater Observatory** lets you look right into a real reef. Circular stairs lead down into an underwater room ringed with windows that actually look right out into the ocean. You see the surface up above and all kinds of fish and underwater plants and corals, all in their natural habitat. It's like snorkeling without getting wet! You can spot live lobsters hiding in the rocks, shimmering silvery waves of giant schools of tiny fish moving as one, and fish hovering just outside the window, gawking at you. Don't get scared as you pass the **Predator Tank**, which is filled with fierce fish—sharks and barracudas. Then there are the **Marine Gardens**, a collection of individual aquariums showcasing sea life up close. Check out the incredibly delicate little seahorses, corals that glow in the dark, burrowing jawfish, and the moray eels. Kids of all ages get a kick out of patting a baby shark at the **Shark Shallows**, feeding stingrays at the **Stingray Pool**, and touching stuff in the "Touch Pond" which has all kinds of sea creatures including some weird ones—a sea cucumber that spits, a worm that goes inside itself when you touch it. If you hate crowds, go later in the day. You'll miss the talks and feedings but you'll be almost alone. *340-775-1555. $18 adult, $9 children 3-12, $58 family pass (2 adults and up to 4 children). Daily 9 a.m.–5:30 p.m. Coki Point.*

DRAKE'S SEAT

Legend has it that Sir Francis Drake used this place as a lookout to spot enemy Spanish fleets. It's now a parking area with a truly spectacular view of Magen's Bay. Vendors selling T-shirts and photographs (in case you didn't bring your camera, I guess) are here during cruise ship hours and there is a delightful donkey decked out in bougainvillaea blossoms that kids can have their picture taken with. Come here early morning or late afternoon to be alone and just absorb the stunning vista. *Route 40.*

FAIRCHILD PARK

A stone pathway and two benches offer spots for rest and relaxation and you can see both sides of the island at the same time from this very tiny, exquisitely peaceful park high up on a mountain. On a clear day, there's a spectacular, almost 360-degree view. *St. Peter Mountain Rd.*

MOUNTAIN TOP

Perched 1547 feet above sea level, this rather touristy spot is one of the highest, easily accessible points on St. Thomas and a good choice for a stunning view overlooking St. Thomas and Magen's Bay and the British Virgin Islands. There's a little restaurant, a number of shops, a bar that specializes in daiquiris, and a long viewing terrace. Bring your camera. By the way, it can be 10 degrees cooler up here than along the shore. *Off of Route 33.*

PARADISE POINT TRAMWAY

Swiss-built gondolas carry you up 700 feet to the top of Flagg Hill and a spectacular view of Charlotte Amalie and the harbor. The trip takes five minutes and stores and a restaurant and bar await you. The outdoor terrace is a perfect place to relax and take in the view. *340-774-9809. Daily 9 a.m.-5 p.m. $12. Across from Havensight.*

SUBMARINE ATLANTIS

Hop into this air-conditioned, 48-passenger submarine for a mile-and-a-half-long underwater tour through the underwater National Wildlife Preserves of Buck Island, just outside of St. Thomas harbor. The journey begins with a 20-minute boat ride out to the 65' submarine. Once you board, the submarine descends to 150 feet. Every seat looks out a 2' wide porthole and the view is spectacular. Sea turtles, parrot fish, sergeant majors, queen angelfish, and yellow-tail snappers swim by. You'll see colorful corals and sponges. You are underwater for about 50 minutes, but the complete excursion takes two hours. *340-776-5650. $72 adults, $36 children (no children under 4). Trips daily Mon.-Sat. Call for schedules, which vary seasonally. Cruise ship dock at Havensight (building #6).*

95

TILLET GARDENS ART CENTER

Stone walkways, shaded by a canopy of spreading tree tops, meander lazily through small gardens at this remarkable and peaceful collection of art galleries and working artist studios.

There is an art gallery, an enamel guild, a goldsmith, a silk-screening studio, a stained glass studio, a hand-painted porcelain and doll workshop, and a Caribbean crafts gallery. When you are ready for a break, stop in at **Polli's** (*340-775-4550*) for a margarita or a meal. It's a good Mexican restaurant.

Internationally-acclaimed artists from around the world perform at **Classics in the Garden**, a series of four Wednesday night concerts held during the winter season.

Arts Alive, a once-a-year event, is held every fall and is a showcase for local artists, sculptors, and designers.

THE BRITISH VIRGIN ISLANDS FOR A DAY

*One of the great things about staying on St. Thomas or St. John is that it is so incredibly easy to drop over to the British Virgin Islands for a day. It's hard to imagine how close these islands are to the USVI until you arrive and realize that you can practically swim to them. Though the BVI look very similar to the USVI—green and remarkably hilly—you'll find that in character, they are astonishingly different. You will definitely feel that you have visited another country—and perhaps even another era. You **must** have a valid passport to visit the BVI.*

THE BVI FROM THE AIR

One of the quickest and most spectacular ways to get an overview of the BVI is to simply fly over them. Take off from the water in downtown Charlotte Amalie with **Seaborne Seaplane Adventures** (*340-773-6442*) for an exciting, 90-minute, narrated "flightseeing" tour. The views are stunning.

THE BVI FROM THE WATER (GROUP TRIPS)

Powerboats are the only boats with enough speed to easily reach many British Virgin Islands in a day, so you get to see almost all the islands from the water, and you get to actually visit several islands. You are taken directly to excellent snorkeling areas and an expert goes in the water with you. From St. Thomas or St. John, **Limnos Charters** (*340-775-3203*) has 53' twin engine, smooth-riding catamarans and takes up to 40 people and **Stormy Petrel** and **Pirate's Penny** (*340-775-7990*) has 42' diesel single engine powerboats and takes up to 12 people. Both trips go along the north side of Tortola and on to the Virgin Gorda Baths and other islands for swimming and snorkeling.

THE BVI FROM THE WATER (PRIVATE CHARTER)

Go on **Rush Hour**, a high-speed 38' cigarette boat with 1000 hp, and at 70 mph, you can get all the way from Red Hook to The Baths on Virgin Gorda in about 45 minutes (that same trip, just one way, takes all day by sail!). Just call **High Performance Charters** (*340-777-7545*) to make arrangements. When you want to customize a snorkeling or beaching or even a hiking trip to the BVI call **Dohm Water Taxi** (*340-775-6501*). Their pilot/ guides are incredibly knowledgeable and can take you places and show you things most people don't know about—like the underwater lava flows off of Tortola. **The Charterboat Center** (*340-775-7990*; from the U.S. *800-866-5714*), located in Red Hook, specializes in trips to the British Virgin Islands and can arrange a variety of powerboat trips, sportfishing trips, day sails, and even weekly charters. If you're not sure what you want, they'll help you decide. Call ahead or stop by their offices.

RENTING YOUR OWN BOAT

This can be a great way to explore the beaches and snorkeling areas of the BVI. From St. Thomas you can reach Jost Van Dyke in 30 minutes, the Caves on Norman Island in 45 minutes, and The Baths on Virgin Gorda in 90 minutes. Everything is closer from St. John. Unless you're an old salt, don't even think of doing this on a really windy day. You'll be wet, scared to death, bounced about, and it will take forever to get anywhere. You must have a passport and clear customs (town dock on Jost Van Dyke, Yacht Harbour on Virgin Gorda, West End or Road Town in Tortola). *See page 88 to rent a boat on St. Thomas, page 131 for St. John.*

PUBLIC FERRIES TO THE BVI

It's a 30-minute trip from Red Hook, St. Thomas to West End, Tortola. From Charlotte Amalie, it's a 45-minute trip to West End and 90 minutes to Road Town, Tortola. Call **Native Son** (*340-774-8685*) or **Smith's Ferry** (*340-775-7292; they also have a Saturday trip to Virgin Gorda*). It's a 30-minute trip from Cruz Bay, St. John to West End, Tortola. Call **Inter-Island** (*340-7766-6597*). On Fridays, Saturdays, and Sundays, Inter-Island (*340-776-6597*) ferries take passengers to the island of Jost Van Dyke from Red Hook, St. Thomas and Cruz Bay, St. John. You'll have time to explore, swim, and visit little beach bars, including Foxy's. Once a month, and twice when there is a blue moon, Inter-Island ferries leave early in the evening for Bomba's famous all-night Full Moon Parties on Tortola.

SECTION II

ST. JOHN

**PLACES TO STAY
RESTAURANTS
BARS
SHOPPING
BEACHES
WATERSPORTS
LANDSPORTS**

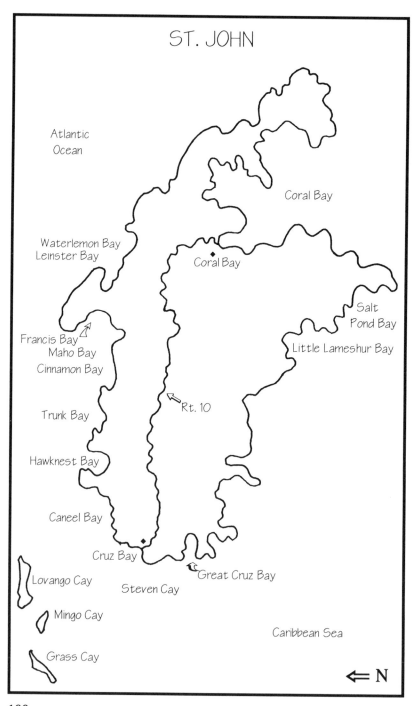

ST. JOHN

Atlantic
Ocean

Coral Bay

Waterlemon Bay
Leinster Bay

Coral Bay

Salt
Pond Bay

Francis Bay
Maho Bay
Cinnamon Bay

Little Lameshur Bay

Rt. 10

Trunk Bay

Hawknest Bay

Caneel Bay

Cruz Bay

Lovango Cay

Great Cruz Bay

Steven Cay

Mingo Cay

Caribbean Sea

Grass Cay

⇐ N

ABOUT ST. JOHN

St. John is a true one-of-a-kind destination and, in a way, has a bit of everything. The island is only 20 square miles and has a population of only 5,000, yet it entices an unusually wide assortment of visitors.

Two-thirds of St. John is part of the U.S. National Park system and the island is extraordinarily untouched. This is an island with terrific hiking trails, numerous exquisite beaches, and superb snorkeling. It's a wonderful place to explore and it's a real outdoor paradise. There are even great campgrounds. However, St. John is also home to a very U.S. mainland-style, full-service resort and to a sophisticated luxury retreat, both of which you never have to leave. There are also a few smaller inns and there are villas to rent all over the island.

St. John is the place to come if you want to spend your days exploring the island by jeep; if you like to hike; if you want to lie on pristine beaches, or find many wonderful snorkeling spots. It's a good island to come to if you want to get away from crowds and do things on your own. St. John is much more isolated than St. Thomas. There's no airport here. You fly to St. Thomas and then take a ferry. Everything on St. John is on a much smaller scale than St. Thomas and it's a much, much quieter island.

St. John is also an island to come to if you want to stay at a luxury resort and be pampered. And it's a place to come if you want to go to little bars, dine outside on gourmet cuisine, or just want to munch a grilled cheese sandwich. You can be as casual or as formal as you want to be.

The "town" of Cruz Bay is about as tiny as you can get and still be a town, yet there are terrific original shops. Restaurants and bars are mostly casual, open-air, and small, yet you'll find very sophisticated cuisine here. The island is extremely hilly but main roads are well-maintained and the drives here are amazing. Roads run through forests and under canopies of trees. They climb alarmingly and drop precipitously, and there are some dicey hairpin curves, but the views and vistas are spectacular, switching back and forth from completely pristine steep green hills to shimmering sea and islands in the distance.

101

A SUGGESTED READING LIST

No assignments, just if you feel like it.

If you are a big reader, James A. Michener's century-spanning tale, *Caribbean.*

For a humorous view of life in paradise, Herman Wouk's *Don't Stop the Carnival.*

For those contemplating a life change, Sidney Hunt's *How to Live in the Caribbean.*

If you're going to Peter Island, Hugh Benjamin's *A Place Like This*—and get Benji to autograph it.

If you're going to the BVI, Pam Acheson's *The Best of the British Virgin Islands, Second Edition.*

For pirate lovers, Fritz Seyfarth's *Pirates of the Virgin Islands.*

For serious readers, Mark Kurlansky's *A Continent of Islands* or Jamaica Kincaid's *A Small Place.*

If you are planning some serious exploring in St. John, Pam Gaffin's *Feet, Fins, and Four-Wheel Drive.*

Jimmy Buffetts' bestseller, *A Pirate Looks at 50.*

If Jost Van Dyke is in your plans, Peter Farrell's *Foxy and Jost Van Dyke.* Get Foxy to sign it.

CHAPTER 8

GREAT ST. JOHN PLACES TO STAY

"I never met a place like this
in my life."
—*Hugh Benjamin*
from *A Place Like This*

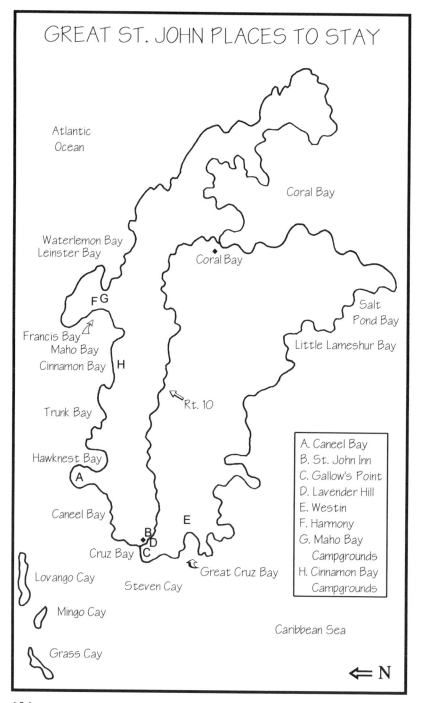

GREAT ST. JOHN PLACES TO STAY

Atlantic Ocean

Coral Bay

Waterlemon Bay
Leinster Bay

Coral Bay

F G

Salt Pond Bay

Francis Bay
Maho Bay
Cinnamon Bay   H

Little Lameshur Bay

Trunk Bay

Rt. 10

Hawknest Bay

A

A. Caneel Bay
B. St. John Inn
C. Gallow's Point
D. Lavender Hill
E. Westin
F. Harmony
G. Maho Bay
    Campgrounds
H. Cinnamon Bay
    Campgrounds

Caneel Bay

E

B
D
Cruz Bay   C

Lovango Cay

Great Cruz Bay

Steven Cay

Mingo Cay

Caribbean Sea

Grass Cay

⇐ N

GREAT ST. JOHN PLACES TO STAY

Over half of St. John is covered by the Virgin Islands National Park and much of the island is completely undeveloped. However, there are a handful of wonderful places to stay on St. John and each one is distinctly different. Some are near the little town of Cruz Bay and some in the Virgin Islands National Park and they run the gamut from full-service resorts to campgrounds. In addition, scattered about all over the island, are neat houses for rent by the week or the month. Rates (except for houses) given below are per night without meals for two people and the range is from the lowest off-season to the highest on-season. There's an additional 8% room tax.

RENTING A HOUSE

People talk about renting villas in the Caribbean, but actually what you are getting most of the time is a house. St. John has a wonderful variety of rental houses to choose from. You can get just about any kind, from a very modest house with simple furnishings and no view and no pool (which is just fine if you plan to spend your days exploring the beaches around the island) to an elegantly furnished four-bedroom villa with a large pool, stunning views, and maid and chef service. You will need to rent a car for your stay, unless you plan to get groceries on the way and never leave.

Rental houses are either on or above a beach, on the water and near a beach, or up in the hills. Although beachfront houses make it delightfully easy to go to the beach, remember that they are generally less private, simply because the beaches are public. Rental houses in the hills can have stunning views, and the higher up you go, the more breathtaking the scene, but bear in mind that St. John is incredibly hilly and roads are very steep. Before you rent, look at a map of St. John and decide what you'd like to be near, such as Cruz Bay or the north shore beaches or Coral Bay. Houses are rented by the week, and rates run all the way from $800 to $8,000.

Caribbean Villas and Resorts, P.O. Box 458, Cruz Bay, 00831. Res: 800-338-0987. Tel: 340-776-6152. Fax: 340-779-4044. www.caribbeanvilla.com.
Catered To, P.O. Box 704, Cruz Bay, 00831. Res: 800-424-6641. Tel: 340-776-6641. Fax: 340-693-8191. cateredto@islands.vi.
Destination St. John Property Management, P.O. Box 8306, Cruz Bay, 00831. Res: 800-562-1901. Tel and fax: 340-779-4647. destinationstjohn.com.

105

CANEEL BAY

If you want understated luxury, and to combine hours of relaxing on very private beaches with exceptional service and elegant cuisine, you can't beat this longtime favorite.

Caneel Bay is on a 170-acre, vaguely hilly peninsula rimmed with seven stunning white sand beaches that are exceptionally private, because most of the property is accessible only to guests. The scenery here is spectacular. Peaceful paths lead to hammocks, benches, and quiet beaches across wide expanses of manicured green lawn radiant with blossoming hibiscus and bougainvillea. From almost anywhere, you can see shades of azure Caribbean waters dotted with hilly, distant islands. Despite the fact that there are 166 units, beaches and paths can be remarkably empty.

Most rooms are in one- and two-story buildings that are beachfront but tucked discretely behind sea grape trees. Others are waterfront or near the tennis courts. Rooms are inviting, expensively but casually decorated, and very comfortable. Some have stonework walls and spacious showers. There are no air-conditioners but ceiling fans and louvered windows truly do keep things cool. Their only drawback is that they do let unwanted noise in. However, you'll find that it is an exquisite sensation to be lulled to sleep by the sound of gently-lapping waves. Meals are a pleasure at all of the restaurants—the atmosphere refined, the service elegant, the cuisine superb. One of the most romantic places on earth to dine is elegant Turtle Bay Estate (even at breakfast, which you can only do on-season).

Don't come here if you want a lot of action or TV or phones (much less computer ports) in your room or opulent jacuzzi bathrooms. Caneel's luxury and elegance is subtle. You'll find it in the fine stonework arch that frames a view from your open-air shower, or the way the beachfront rooms have splendid water views yet are hidden in the sea grapes, so as not to spoil the untouched feel of the beach. This is one of the few luxury resorts left where you can actually leave the real world behind. Guests young and old come back year after year because, for them, this kind of escape is one of the most relaxing and restorative experiences there is.

4 restaurants, bar, pool, 11 tennis courts, 7 beaches (excellent snorkeling), massage, fitness center, hiking, shop, cell phones on request, office center with computer and fax. No children under 8 Jan.-Mar. Special packages. 166 units. P.O. Box 720, Cruz Bay, 00831. Res: 800-928-8889. Tel: 340-776-6111. Fax: 340-693-8280. www.rosewood-hotels.com. $250-$900.

GALLOWS POINT SUITE RESORT

Stay here for spectacular views and superb snorkeling right out front. Cruz Bay is just a short walk away.

The land that wraps around the southern end of Cruz Bay ends with a promontory known as Gallows Point. Fourteen grey, two-story, quadraplex condominiums are clustered here. From the water they appear almost too close to each other, but from the inside, tall, louvered doors completely fold back and showcase sensational views of turquoise waters and nearby islands and you completely forget that anyone could be right next door. All units have a separate bedroom, fully-equipped kitchen, a living/dining area with a sleeper sofa, ceiling fans, and patio or balcony. Some bedrooms are air-conditioned. Second-floor units are more spacious and have high ceilings over the living areas, loft bedrooms with a half-bath, and more dramatic views. All units have tile floors and are furnished in rattan and tropical prints. The pool and beach are quite tiny but the snorkeling is really superb all along the shore heading away from Cruz Bay. Ellington's, the on-site restaurant, is well-respected and its third floor bar is one of the best spots on the island to watch the sun set and to try and catch the green flash.

Restaurant, bar, small pool, tiny beach, gift shop and activities center. 60 units. P.O. Box 58, Cruz Bay, 00831. Res: 800-348-8444. Tel: 340-776-6434. Fax: 340-776-6080. www.gallowspoint.com. $175-$365.

LAVENDER HILL ESTATES

This small condominium complex offers comfortable apartment living with a pool, and you can walk to town.

Apartments are in two buildings that peek out from the top of tropical foliage on a hillside overlooking Cruz Bay. There are eight one-bedroom apartments and four penthouse apartments. All units have a separate bedroom, a living-dining area, a fully-equipped kitchen, and a TV/VCR. Units also have air-conditioning and ceiling fans. Each condominium is privately owned and decor varies, but generally you can count on tile floors, rattan furniture, and pastel prints. Long, wrap-around balconies catch the tropical breezes and are perfect spots to read or just gaze at the view and watch the harbor traffic in the distance. A nice size pool is nestled in between the two buildings. Cruz Bay restaurants and shops are just a short walk down the hill.

Pool. 12 units. P.O. 567, Cruz Bay, 00831. Res: 800-348-8444. Tel: 340-776-6969. Fax: 340-779-4486. www.lavenderhill.net. $140-$255.

HARMONY

Kids and grown ups get a kick out of this place, which is built entirely out of recycled materials.

Nestled among the trees above Maho Bay are these delightfully contemporary, comfortable duplex units built entirely out of recycled materials. You'd never guess what everything once was, even if you look very closely! Just for starters, the roof is made out of recycled cardboard, the doormat was fashioned out of melted old tires, the shiny white walls were once newspapers, the shower tiles are created out of crushed light bulbs, and the outdoor furniture was originally soda bottles! Even some of the decor was once something else, like the throw rugs woven from plastic milk bottles. Don't be frightened. Nothing even vaguely resembles what it once was and these units are very comfortable and attractive. Upstairs units are studios with cathedral ceilings and downstairs units have a separate bedroom and standard-height ceilings. All have kitchenettes (low-voltage refrigerator, of course), spacious decks, and spectacular views. There's a beautiful beach down the hill. This is one of ecologist Stanley Selengut's marvelous brainstorms.

12 units. P.O. Box 310, Cruz Bay, 00831. Res: 800-392-9004. Tel: 340-776-6240. Fax: 340-776-6504. www.maho.org.com. $105-$195.

ST. JOHN INN

This intimate, rather elegant little inn has its own pool and is just a short walk from Cruz Bay.

California meets the Caribbean at this appealing inn, which the owners have imbued with their West Coast style. The outside is the color of terra cotta and the trim is a dark green. Inside, Ralph Lauren linens, wrought iron four-poster beds, and wardrobe armoires add a dash of elegance to this small inn. All units have a phone and TV/VCR. Junior suites also have kitchenettes. Some units look out to the pool and three have ocean views. There's a lovely courtyard with a swimming pool surrounded by a redwood deck and a bar (with a giant TV screen, which may dismay some). This is a good place to watch the sunset. The inn also offers guests daily boat trips on the 43' motor yacht Hollywood Waltz. The owners will happily help you arrange for car rentals and any island activities. The inn's location is wonderful. You can easily walk to Cruz Bay shops, restaurants, and bars.

Bar, pool. 12 units. P.O. Box 37, Cruz Bay, 00831. Res: 800-666-7688. Tel and fax: 340-693-8688. $100-$180.

WESTIN RESORT, ST. JOHN

Busy and bustling, this full-service resort is the most stateside-like spot on St. John and both honeymooners and families flock here.

This resort is set on 47 acres that sweep down to a long crescent of white sand and look out to a harbor of sailboats gently rocking at anchor. Low-rise buildings with magenta roofs cascade down to the beach, separated by strips of green lawn, rows of palm trees, well-tended beds of purple flowers that match the roofs, and broad brick walkways. Rooms are spacious and contemporary. Walls are painted in soft colors, with deeper hued woodwork and doors and prints hang on the walls. All rooms have mini-bars, TV and in-room movies, and large bathrooms. The closer you are to the beach, the better the water view.

Upstairs in the main reception building and open to the breezes is the light and airy Coccoloba Grill, the resort's fancy dinner restaurant. Down the hill and facing the beach is the Beach Cafe & Bar, which is open for breakfast, lunch, and dinner plus a lavish Sunday brunch. There's a very casual lunch and snack spot near the pool, and a bar right next to the pool. There's also a complete deli back behind the tennis courts where you can buy sandwiches, cookies, a small selection of groceries, and daily specials. Room service is offered round the clock, including pizza, to munch on while you watch one of the current in-room movies.

Activities center around the 1,200-foot beach and the quarter-acre, geometric-shaped pool, complete with two jacuzzis and a small waterfall. The watersports center offers windsurfing, snorkeling, jet skiing, plus fishing, sailing, and scuba trips.

The beach and the pool keep children busy but there is also an outstanding Kids Club which offers children ages three to twelve a full range of indoor and outdoor activities. It's open for half-day, full-day, and evening sessions and kids learn island arts and crafts, find out all about iguanas, and get involved in beach activities and volleyball games. On the far side of the entrance, nestled among trees and thick planting, there are also 96 vacation villas available for rent. Some have their own private pools.

3 restaurants, 3 bars, pool, beach, 6 tennis courts, fitness center, massage, 2 gift shops. Special packages. 285 units. P.O. Box 8310, Cruz Bay, 00831. Res: 800-937-8461. Tel: 340-693-8000. Fax: 340-779-4500. www.westin.com. $220-$575, suites more.

CINNAMON BAY CAMPGROUND

Here, rustic cottages, tents, and bare sites are hidden in the trees just minutes from a gorgeous white sand beach.

Cinnamon Bay, which is in the Virgin Islands National Park, is St. John's longest beach. Set back against the hills and concealed among the tropical foliage, is this superb campground. There are three types of accommodations, all within a two-minute walk from the beach and all with picnic table and charcoal grill. You have the choice of screen-lined, 15' by 15' "cottages," with electric lights, ceiling fan, four twin beds and linens (changed twice weekly), propane gas stove, ice chest, cooking and eating utensils; canvas 10' by 14' tents on a solid floor, with a gas lantern, cots, linens (changed twice weekly), propane gas stove, ice chest, cooking and eating utensils; and bare sites, which can handle one large tent or two smaller tents. Bathrooms are nearby and there are public phones, a message center, safe deposit boxes, and lockers. Breakfast and lunch are served at a snack bar and the open-air restaurant Tree Lizards dishes up seafood, barbecues, and vegetarian delights every evening and even West Indian music on-season. The Beach Shop and Activities Deck arranges snorkeling, windsurfing, sea kayaking, and sailboat rentals, plus sailing cruises and scuba and snorkeling trips. Winter months fill up as far as a year in advance.

Restaurant, snack bar, beach, grocery store, gift shop. 126 units. P.O. Box 720, Cruz Bay, 00831. Res: 800-539-9998. Tel: 340-776-6330. Fax: 340-776-6458. www.cinnamonbay.com. Cottages 105-$120, tents $80, bare sites $20. MAP rates also available.

MAHO BAY CAMPGROUND

Come here for hillside camping on a small but beautiful beach.

Fourteen acres of forested hillside rise up from a classic, white sand beach seemingly undisturbed, yet here and there, clusters of open-sided, 16' by 16' tent cottages exist among the trees. It's amazing how very undisturbed the land is. Stairs and elevated walkways wind around trunks, disturbing nothing. Opened in the early '70s, this was Stanley Selengut's first ecological venture on St. John and it is still going strong. Beds, tables, chairs, propane stoves, and cooking utensils are provided. Some tents have superb water views. An activities desk offers sailing, snorkeling, windsurfing, and other watersports.

113 units. P.O. Box 310, Cruz Bay, 00831. Res: 800-392-9004. Tel: 340-693-6596. Fax: 340-776-6504. www.maho.org. $25-$125.

110

HISTORICAL ATTRACTIONS ON ST. JOHN

ANNABERG SUGAR MILL

This sugar mill operated well into the late 1800s and these ruins are well-preserved and a delight to visit. The National Park brochure identifies the buildings, describes how sugar was produced, and even names fruit trees. The view of the British Virgin Islands from here is superb. Sometimes there are historical re-enactments. *340-776-6201. Rt. 20, near Leinster Bay.*

ELAINE IONE SPRAUVE LIBRARY & MUSEUM

Built in 1757, this former great house is now a library and a museum, with a small collection of Indian pottery and artifacts from ancient and colonial days. There are permanent exhibits on Danish West Indian history, natural history, and arts and crafts. Come here also to see ever-changing exhibits of work by local artists. *Open weekdays 9-5. 340-776-6359. Cruz Bay.*

IVAN JADAN MUSEUM

Ivan Jadan, considered one of the greatest Russian tenors of all time, spent his last 40 years on St. John. He died in 1995 and his wife has lovingly created this museum, a tribute to the classical singer's 92-year life and love for music. Historic photos, documents, and items are on display and there are numerous books you are welcome to read and you can listen to some of his performances, too, including the posthumously-released CD, "Songs of the Heart." *Mon.-Sat. 9-11, 4-6, and by appointment. 340-776-6423. Genip St., Cruz Bay.*

WHAT TO DO
ON ST. JOHN

St. John is a great place to be.
What can you do there?

You can hike on trails,
head to beautiful beaches,
follow the underwater snorkel trail
at Trunk Bay,
wander around the little town
of Cruz Bay,
browse through very original shops in one of the
prettiest shopping spots
in the Caribbean, Mongoose Junction,
look for a real mongoose,
rent a car and drive around the island (take
Centerline Road in at least one direction to see
spectacular views),
have an elegant brunch at Caneel,
have frozen drinks in funky bars,
take the Reef Bay Trail and see petroglyphs,
watch fabulous phosphorescent trails on a night
snorkel.

CHAPTER 9

GREAT ST. JOHN RESTAURANTS & BARS

"Only Irish coffee provides in a single glass
all four essential food groups:
alcohol, caffeine, sugar, and fat."

—*Alex Levine*

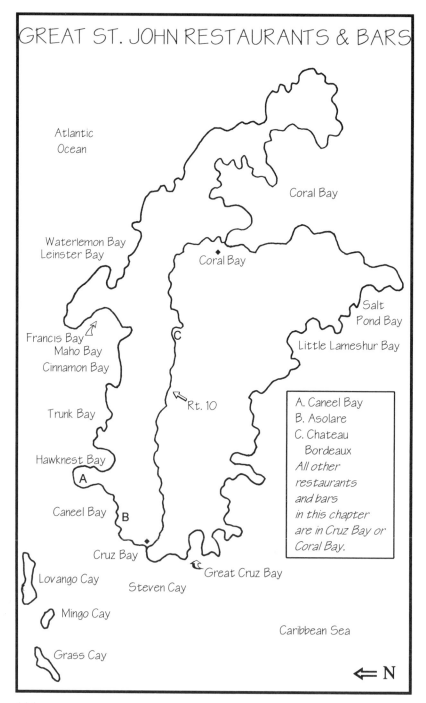

GREAT ST. JOHN RESTAURANTS & BARS

Atlantic
Ocean

Coral Bay

Waterlemon Bay
Leinster Bay

Coral Bay

Salt
Pond Bay

Francis Bay
Maho Bay
Cinnamon Bay

Little Lameshur Bay

C

Rt. 10

Trunk Bay

A. Caneel Bay
B. Asolare
C. Chateau
   Bordeaux
*All other
restaurants
and bars
in this chapter
are in Cruz Bay or
Coral Bay.*

Hawknest Bay

A

Caneel Bay
B

Cruz Bay

Great Cruz Bay

Lovango Cay
Steven Cay

Mingo Cay

Caribbean Sea

Grass Cay

⇐ N

GREAT ST. JOHN RESTAURANTS & BARS

One of the most magical and enchanting features of the Caribbean is the ability to have elegant meals on terraces that are open to the outdoors, to combine a sophisticated and refined style of dining with soft breezes and romantic nighttime scenery—sparkling stars, rising moons, twinkling distant lights.

While St. Thomas restaurants generally have sophisticated interiors, even the finest St. John restaurants rely on the outdoor scenery and island breezes to create an inviting background for an elegant meal. In fact, it is possible to walk by an excellent restaurant on St. John in the afternoon and see only a stack of plastic chairs on a concrete floor, and a padlock and chain draped around the kitchen door. You just know that place must be closed for good. Yet return in the evening, and you'll find tablecloths, candlelight, and glistening wine buckets.

All restaurants below are open daily for lunch and dinner unless otherwise stated. Bear in mind that, off-season, hours and days of operation may vary and it is wise to call ahead. On-season, it's a good idea to make a dinner reservation at the fancier restaurants. Cruz Bay spots are all within easy walking distance of each other.

ST. JOHN'S FINEST RESTAURANTS

ASOLARE
The modest lattice and stonework entrance belies the stunning scenery that awaits you once inside. This small, elegant restaurant is set high up on a hillside in a restored stone house and the entire front looks out to a spectacular panorama of azure waters and distant islands. At night, the twinkling lights of St. Thomas are magical. The view alone would be worth the visit, but you'll find that the exquisitely-presented, contemporary Asian cuisine is equally outstanding. You might start with lobster and daikon with a watermelon salsa, or frog legs rubbed with wasabi and pan-seared and served with a vegetable curry sauce and sticky rice, or stone-seared carpaccio. Good dinner choices include an excellent crispy Peking duck, salmon with sauteed vegetables and a wasabi-passion fruit sauce, and a grilled filet of beef with angel hair potatoes, stir fry vegetables, and a ginger-zinfandel sauce. *No lunch. 340-779-4747. A two-minute cab ride from Cruz Bay on Caneel Hill. $$-$$$.*

115

PANINI BEACH

White latticework and yellow flowers mark the waterfront setting of this superb Northern Italian restaurant. Although there are tables inside, romantics surely will want to dine outside, with the beach a step away, the waters of Cruz Bay softly lapping, and the twinkling nighttime lights. Salads are large and also outstandingly good. Try the baby greens tossed with pears, gorgonzola, and toasted walnuts or the Balsamic Onion Bread Salad with roasted onions and peppers, currants, pine nuts, and spinach. Excellent main course choices are the penne with sausage and mascarpone, the capellini with basil and sun-dried tomatoes, and the seared tuna encrusted with pepper on a bed of caramelized onions. There are also several thin-crusted pizzas. Check out the daily specials, which sometimes include a superb orecchiette dish. Owner/chef team Joe Guarise and Janet Kleiner want to please, so ask for what you want, even if it is not on the menu. Excellent wines are quite reasonably priced. On-season, pizzas, salads, and panini (Italian sandwiches) are offered at lunch and pizzas and frittatas at Sunday Brunch. *340-693-9119. Wharfside Village. $$.*

CANEEL BAY TERRACE

For elegant buffets with outstanding selections—for lunch, dinner, and even breakfast—you can't beat Caneel Bay Terrace. The buffets here are among the very best anywhere. The cuisine is of the finest quality, the al fresco setting is peaceful, and the service gracious and refined. Well-spaced tables look out to a bay and this is a superb place to come when you feel like a long, relaxed, and elegant meal. There are numerous hot and cold selections plus cooked-to-order choices, all beautifully presented. *Buffets are breakfast and lunch Mon.-Sat., brunch Sun., dinner Mon. and Fri. Reservations for dinner essential. 340-776-6111. On Rte. 20, five minutes north of Cruz Bay. $$$.*

CHATEAU BORDEAUX

This is just about the highest place you can drive to on St. John and the attentive service and gourmet cuisine at this restaurant are a perfect match for the panoramic vista. Try to get here before dark so you can see the stunning sunsets and the truly amazing view of the British Virgin Islands. Appetizers include a spicy Caribbean gumbo, escargot in puff pastry, and gnocchi with pine nuts and brie butter cream. There's also a wonderful spinach salad. For entrees, the pork tenderloin stuffed with andouille sausage, apples, and walnuts or the Caribbean lobster tail or the fresh tuna pan-seared with a wasabi-teriyaki glaze are excellent choices. Driving here in the dark is not for the faint of heart, so consider taking a cab unless you know the road. Lunch is served on the outside deck only and the simple menu includes cheeseburgers and hamburgers. There's a neat little gift shop that is open from 10 a.m. to 4 p.m. *Reservations for dinner essential. 340-776-6611. Centerline Rd. at Carolina Hill. $$-$$$.*

PARADISO

Stonework walls and French doors mark the entrance to this large and appealing restaurant. Inside, high ceilings, pastel walls, framed art, tropical plants, and hardwood floors create a sophisticated and upscale background for fine cuisine. Smoked bacon risotto, goat cheese ravioli, the beer-battered shrimp, or the roasted garlic Caesar salad are good choices for starters. Then move on to grilled veal medallions, pan-roasted sea bass with cannelini beans and a corn-sherry-shallot vinaigrette, or a sirloin with portobello mushrooms, roasted peppers, and asparagus. On cool nights, the brick balcony, lined mostly with tables for two, is a romantic choice. *Sometimes closed Sun. No lunch. 340-693-8899. Mongoose Junction. $$-$$$.*

STONE TERRACE

Broad steps lead up a rather grand stonework entrance to this pleasant al fresco restaurant with stonework walls and arched wooden doors. Tables are set on a terrace and look out to the harbor. The ambitious menu changes periodically but might include mushrooms stuffed with escargot and boursin, oysters Rockefeller, or Thai duck salad with a spicy coconut dressing. The rack of lamb with a pistachio crust is a house specialty but the passion fruit chicken on macadamia risotto and the filet mignon with lobster salsa are also good choices. *No lunch. 340-693-9370. Across from Wharfside Village. $$-$$$.*

CASUAL CRUZ BAY FAVORITES

FISH TRAP

Locals and visitors keep this popular restaurant full year-round. Tables are in several open-air rooms and on balconies and there's never an empty one. Fish lovers have a hard time choosing between the five or six "fishes of the day" and shrimp, scallops, or lobster. Seafood choices are also paired with steaks, and there are several pasta dishes, including a vegetarian primavera. The conch fritters and Fish Trap chowder both make fine appetizers. *Closed Mon. No lunch. 340-693-9994. Near south end of Wharfside Village. $$.*

LA TAPA

White stucco walls, arched doorways, and roughly-hewn, dark wooden tables create a decidedly Spanish atmosphere at this cozy spot. Soups include potato and leek and a spicy gazpacho. Salads range from superb, homemade mozzarella with tomatoes and basil to a sumptuous cashew-breaded goat cheese on a bed of greens. Excellent entrees include the tuna with papaya-avocado salsa and the filet mignon with a gorgonzola, caramelized onion, and port sauce. But it's also fun to just order one tapa after another. Brie, Kalamata olives, chorizo, and smoked salmon are some of the best. Tables outside can be noisy. *Closed Sun. No lunch. 340-693-7755. Across from Chase bank. $$.*

LIME INN

Plants hang from the ceiling and the latticework at this casual, open-air, and incredibly popular spot tucked in the back of an esplanade. Crowds come here nightly for grilled fish, N.Y. strip, and Caribbean lobster. Wednesday night is the incredibly popular, all-you-can-eat Shrimp Feast (no reservations). Quiches, soups, salads, burgers, and sandwiches are available at lunch. *Closed Sun. No lunch Sat. 340-776-6425. Lemon Tree Mall. $$.*

ZOZO'S RISTORANTE

Dine indoors, with windows open to the breezes, or on the terrace of this charming northern Italian restaurant. Start with a tasty tower of eggplant and melted cheeses or black mussels in white wine. Then move on to the rigatoni with hot sausage or the basil-infused linguini with calamari or try the savory zuppe de pesce (here served on angel hair) or the stuffed veal chop or osso bucco. *Closed Wed. No lunch. 340-693-9200. Across from Chase Bank. $$.*

PUSSERS

It seems that everyone stops by Pussers at least once. Crowds head here for the congenial atmosphere and appealing decor, the famous Pussers' Painkiller, and for good food. Tables are both inside and on the breezy second-floor terrace which looks out over the boats anchored in Cruz Bay. Steaks, sandwiches, grilled chicken, conch fritters, chicken roti, chowders, and more are on the menu. *340-693-8489. Wharfside Village.*

CRUZ BAY LUNCH (AND BREAKFAST) BREAKS
CHILI BILLY'S

This snug, upstairs, open-air, and very casual hillside spot serves hamburgers cheeseburgers, large salads, soups, and sandwiches, including an excellent club. Scrambled eggs, omelets, Monkeybread French toast, and other breakfast items are available until closing. If it's full, have a seat at the small indoor counter. *8 a.m-2 p.m. 340-693-8708. Across from the lumberyard. $.*

J. J.'S TEXAS COAST CAFE

This is a great, ultra-casual place to rest your feet and have coffee or a frozen drink or an ice cold beer and a bite to eat while you watch the people come and go from the ferry dock. Tables are crowded together on a little gravel terrace and shaded by Lowenbrau umbrellas. The basic U.S./Tex-Mex menu features the Texas Trash Basket (fried cheese, fried veggies, and french fries), Texas-style chili, enchiladas, nachos, cheeseburgers, and a good grilled cheese sandwich. Breakfast includes huevos rancheros. Inside are more tables and a bar. *Opens 8 a.m. 340-776-6908. Across the park from ferry dock. $.*

MARGARITA'S MEXICAN EATERY & CANTINA
Come here for Mexican cuisine with a vegetarian twist. Oversized tacos, sizzling fajitas, and spicy burritos are on the menu and just about anything you want can be made totally vegetarian. Keep a look out for the balloon man, who is busy blowing up colorful balloons. *11:30 a.m.-9:30 p.m. Closed Mon. 340-693-8400. Just south of Mongoose Junction. $.*

CRUZ BAY BARS AND ENTERTAINMENT
DOCKSIDE PUB
People just off the ferry generally head straight here for an icy cold beer before they catch a cab, rent a car, or decide what they are going to do next. *340-693-8855. Just to the right as you come off the ferry dock.*

DUFFY'S LOVE SHACK
This long-time St.Thomas favorite has finally expanded to St. John and it sports the same thatched-roof bar and is the place to come for a huge array of tropical drinks, frozen drinks, and flaming drinks. They serve food, too. *340-776-6065. Behind Sparky's.*

ELLINGTON'S
People flock to the open-air, third-floor bar here at the end of the day to watch the extraordinary Caribbean sunsets. During certain times of the year, the sun sets in the water instead of behind another island and you can actually catch the famous green flash. *340-693-8490. Gallow's Point.*

GECKO GAZEBO
Pause in between shops at this charming, little outdoor bar. Check out the daily drink specials and the munchies menu. *340-693-8340. Mongoose Junction.*

J.J.'S TEXAS COAST CAFE
This is a pretty ordinary bar but the beer is icy cold and you can count on the TV being set to whatever stateside sports event you don't want to miss. *340-776-6908. Across the park from the ferry dock.*

LA TAPA
The bar is tiny but they make marvelous margaritas the old-fashioned way (from scratch) and you can wile away the evening here ordering one tapa after another. Or come early for "Tapas Hours" (3:30 p.m. to 6:30 p.m. Monday through Friday) and sample various tapas (at slightly reduced prices) served with dipping sauces and chutneys. There's jazz some evenings. *340-693-7755. Near Chase Bank.*

119

LIME INN

Way back in the left corner of this popular restaurant is a small, but equally popular bar. *Closed Sun. 340-776-6425. Lemon Tree Mall.*

QUIET MON

Posters of Irish writers and shelves full of books decorate this casual upstairs restaurant and bar, which features fine Irish whiskeys, stouts, and a good selection of beers and ales. Fridays from 4 p.m. to 6 p.m. a quartet plays Irish celtic music. Take your drink to the outside balcony if you want to people watch. *340-779-4799. Across from Chase Bank.*

PARADISO

The wood glistens at the long and handsome bar in this popular, upscale restaurant. *Closed Sun. 340-693-8899. Mongoose Junction.*

PUSSERS

Try a famous Pussers' Painkiller at the third-floor Crow's Nest at sunset time, or inside at the busy bar. *340-693-8489. Wharfside Village.*

WOODY'S SEAFOOD SALOON

Locals fill this joint up inside and out every afternoon for happy hour, which actually runs from 3 p.m. to 6 p.m. Try an order of shark bites or fritters. *340-779-4625. Across from Chase Bank.*

CORAL BAY RESTAURANTS & BARS
SECRETS OF CORAL BAY

This appealing restaurant is right on the water and you dine to the sounds of the waves. For appetizers try the calamari or littleneck clams. For the main course the beef filet, grilled tuna, or tender snapper are good choices. There are also chicken and spinach pizzas. On the lunch menu is a great Philly cheese steak. Breezes keep it cool and in the winter you might even want to bring a sweater. *Closed Mon. 340-693-5630. $$.*

SHIPWRECK LANDING

Dine casually al fresco on burgers, Caesar salad, Greek salad, fish 'n' chips, taco salad, pasta specials here. *Bands Wed.-Thurs. eves. 340-693-5640. $-$$.*

SKINNY LEGS BAR AND RESTAURANT

Come to this casual, popular spot for a grilled portobella mushroom sandwich, or a turkey and swiss cheese sandwich, or great chili dogs, burgers, and grilled fish. Friday nights, there's often a band. *340-779-4982. $.*

A FEW FACTS ABOUT ST. JOHN

St. John is about the size of Manhattan.

Over two-thirds of the island is a National Park.

All beaches on St. John are open to the public.

St. John is about nine miles long and just under 1300 feet above sea level at its highest point, Bordeaux Mountain.

St. John is about the same distance from St. Thomas as it is from Tortola or Norman Island in the British Virgins.

It was first inhabited by Arawak indians moving up from South America.

And "discovered" by Columbus on his second voyage in 1493.

Although it sometimes seems like too many cars on the island now, there weren't any cars on the island at all until the 1950s.

St. John is home to about 5,000 residents and a vacationing destination for many, many more.

ALWAYS . . .

Always be nicer to people than necessary.

Always lock your hotel room and rental car.

Always have a hat, bandanna, or something to cover your head during the day.

Always remember to keep left when you are driving.

Always look right, first, and then left before crossing the street.

Always put on some sun screen before going outside during the day.

Always greet people and ask how they are doing before conducting any "business."

Always remember the sometimes slower pace you encounter is part of island charm.

Always snorkel with at least one other person.

CHAPTER 10

GREAT ST. JOHN SHOPPING, OUTDOOR ACTIVITIES

"The race is not always to the swift,
nor the battle to the strong;
but that's the way to bet it."
—*Damon Runyon*

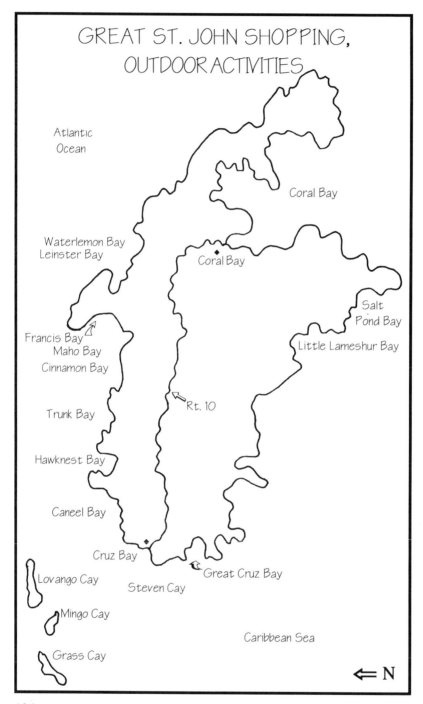

GREAT ST. JOHN SHOPPING,
OUTDOOR ACTIVITIES

Atlantic
Ocean

Coral Bay

Waterlemon Bay
Leinster Bay

Coral Bay

Salt
Pond Bay

Francis Bay
Maho Bay

Little Lameshur Bay

Cinnamon Bay

Rt. 10

Trunk Bay

Hawknest Bay

Caneel Bay

Cruz Bay

Lovango Cay

Great Cruz Bay

Steven Cay

Mingo Cay

Caribbean Sea

Grass Cay

N

GREAT ST. JOHN SHOPPING

Shopping on St. John is a pleasure. Shops are all in downtown Cruz Bay, they are easy to find, and there are many superb, one-of-a-kind places. Plus, none get ridiculously crowded the way stores do in Charlotte Amalie. Shops are clustered together in three areas. Mongoose Junction, is a five-minute walk north of the ferry dock, and its beautiful stonework walls and arches make it one of the prettiest shopping areas anywhere. Wharfside Village is right on the water, south of the ferry dock, and anchored by three levels of Pusser's bars and restaurants. In between, "in the middle of town," is a loose collection of stores. You can cover all of Cruz Bay on foot in about an hour or half a day, depending on what kind of shopper you are. Some of the best shops are described below.

MONGOOSE JUNCTION

BAMBOULA

Handsome armoires and cabinets showcase a mix of clothing, textiles, and art. You'll find comfy, stylish island clothing for women—long, loose cotton or rayon dresses, slinky camisoles, silk sweaters, even shoes; island shirts and shorts for men; and, further on into the store, sheets, bedspreads, cotton throws, primitive art, and woven baskets. *340-693-8699.*

BATIK KITAB

Stop here for the batiks by St. John artist Judy Aradi. She focuses on Caribbean images and works on silk, cotton, linen, and paper. *340-776-6385.*

BEST OF BOTH WORLDS

Creativity is at its best in this terrific gallery, which will ship anything anywhere. Look for fine oil and watercolor paintings, metal and wire sculptures, silver and gold jewelry, some really whimsical art, and superbly restful waterfalls (yes, these can be shipped home, too). Be sure to look up to catch all the great things hanging from the ceiling, and check out the upstairs, where there's more of everything. *340-693-7005.*

BIG PLANET ADVENTURE OUTFITTERS

Get ready for anything you might want to do outdoors with a stop in this huge store, which features swimwear, sportswear, active wear, sundresses, sunglasses, footwear, backpacks, luggage, and accessories from Patagonia, Teva, Jams World, Timberland, and Birkenstock for everyone in the whole family. *340-776-6638.*

125

BOUGAINVILLEA

Wares are displayed outside and in at this spot, which offers a small selection of upscale, stylish women's clothing (shirts, dresses, pants, shoes, sweaters) and a potpourri of appealing gift items. *340-693-7190.*

CANVAS FACTORY

Practical, durable canvas is the specialty here, fashioned into handsome hats, briefcases, purses, and luggage in all sizes. *340-776-6196.*

CLOTHING STUDIO

Watch artists hand paint everything from bathing suits to hats, t-shirts, sundresses, and cover-ups at this popular shop. *340-776-6585.*

FABRIC MILL

Shelves are filled with bedspreads, pillows, table linens, sarongs, fabric by the yard—all in beautiful colors and prints—plus cookbooks and rugs. It's hard to resist buying something here for the house. *340-776-6194.*

MAPes MONDe

Come here for elegant books by Virgin Island publisher MAPes MONDe, books on the Caribbean, fine reproductions of historic Caribbean maps, original paintings, prints of flowers, and greeting cards. *340-779-4545.*

R&I PATTON GOLDSMITHING

Owners Rudy and Irene Patton design the highly original gold and silver jewelry you'll see at this superb jewelry store. Look for delicate seahorse earrings, a trio of dancing lizards on a pin, a charm bracelet of different tropical fish, a sea turtle pendant, plus unique chains and rings. Tahitian pearls, gemstones, and opal inlay are also specialties. *340-776-6548.*

WHARFSIDE VILLAGE

FREEBIRD

This little shop is a good spot to pick up incense sticks, toe rings, ear swords and shackles, and New Age reading material. They also sell sterling silver and gold jewelry and the pale blue larimar stone. *340-693-8625.*

ISOLA

Don't miss this wonderful shop, with its appealing, eclectic mix—Sloop Jones hand-painted dresses and sweaters, silk-covered flax eye pillows, gentle wind chimes, scented candles, neat hats, roomy purses, slender ceramic bud vases, colorful fabrics, bright table napkins, and so much more—all beautifully arranged. The more you look, the more you see. *340-779-4212.*

PUSSER'S LTD.

Come here for Pusser's famous rum, in bottles and fancy decanters; nautical memorabilia; books about the Caribbean; plus Pusser's comfortable, casual clothing—pants, sweaters, T-shirts, sweatshirts, shorts, shirts, bathing suits—for the whole family. *340-693-8489.*

SHADY DAYS

Squinting from the bright, tropical glare of the Caribbean sun? Head here for a fancy pair of designer shades, such as Oakley, Revo, Maui Jim, and Persol. This is also the best source for cigars on St. John. *340-693-7625.*

MIDDLE OF TOWN

PINK PAPAYA

Pink is just the beginning at this colorful shop, which features the work of St. John artist M. Lisa Etre! Just about everything here is in bright pastel solids and prints: oversize pillows, table linens, hand-painted dinnerware, ceramic bowls, coffee cups, stained glass ornaments, wacky sculptures, and even the colorful books and the Caribbean art displayed on the walls. *340-693-8535. From ferry dock, walk inland 2 blocks to Chase bank and walk right.*

SILVERLINING

This tiny shop features lovely, handcrafted jewelry—bracelets, earrings, rings—plus appealing interesting pottery. *340-693-7766. From ferry, walk inland 2 blocks to Chase bank and walk left.*

SPARKY'S

For the latest stateside newspaper, a paperback, film, sunscreen, candy bars, a T-shirt, or a bottle of liquor, wine, or champagne, everyone heads here. *340-776-6284. West side of the park.*

CANEEL BAY RESORT SHOP

Definitely worth a stop is this terrific resort shop, stocked with resortwear for men and women, a superb selection of women's swimwear, jewelry, pottery, beautiful hand-painted glasses by Shannon, current paperbacks, books on the islands, plus colorful T-shirts, sweatshirts, glassware, and beach towels emblazoned with the famous Caneel petroglyph logo. *340-776-6111.*

OUTDOOR ACTIVITIES

St. John is an outdoor paradise, above the water and below. There are terrific hiking and horseback riding trails, stunning beaches, calm swimming waters, and spectacular snorkeling. Luckily, much of the island is protected by the U.S. National Park Service. The Virgin Islands National Park includes just over half of St. John plus almost all of the north shore beaches, some south shore beaches, and the waters around these beaches.

LANDSPORTS

BIRD WATCHING

In winter months, bird lovers head to the Francis Bay Trail where they hope to spot a West Indian whistling duck, yellow-billed cuckoo, and some of the other more than 160 species of birds that live in this area.

HIKING

The National Park Service maintains over 20 hiking trails that lead through mountain forests and dry cactus and along old plantation roads to extraordinary beaches, overlooks with breathtaking views of the sea and neighboring islands, and historic sugar plantation ruins. Trails vary greatly in degree of difficulty and length and range from 10 minutes to three hours. Pick up a copy of the VI National Park Trail Guide (count on trail times taking a little longer than stated) and be sure to bring plenty of drinking water with you. *340-776-6201.* *National Park Visitor Center, Cruz Bay, north of the park (if it's not there, then they've finally finished renovating the real center which is down the road across from Mongoose Junction).*

GUIDED HIKES

The National Park Service offers guided hikes down steep Reef Bay Trail, which includes a visit to sugar mill ruins and to ancient petroglyphs, and ends at a beach. Although signs along the way make this an easy trip to do on your own, the guided trip returns via boat while everyone else has a steep, two-mile hike back up the trail! *340-776-6201. Call for reservations as soon as you know your vacation plans (hikes fill up fast). Mon. and Thurs., $15 per person.*

HORSEBACK AND DONKEY RIDING

Go horseback or donkey riding along scenic trails up into the mountains or down to the beach. You can even go swimming with your horse! Carolina Corral Trail Rides offers two-hour rides, half-day rides, and sunset and full moon rides. *340-693-5778. $55-$90.*

BEACHES AND SNORKELING

HAWKSNEST BAY

The reef is close to shore at this narrow beach which gets crowded because it's so close to Cruz Bay. **Snorkeling:** Three reefs run out from the beach. Look for squid, damselfish, all kinds of angelfish, flat worms, anemones. *North shore.*

TRUNK BAY

Trunk Bay is a calm bay bordered by a gorgeous sweep of white sand fringed with sea grape and palm trees which makes every list of the world's most beautiful beaches, so, unfortunately, it's no secret. Cruise ships send taxiloads of passengers here. It is still worth a visit, but to avoid the crowds come in the early morning or late afternoon. **Snorkeling:** There's a 225-foot, underwater, marked snorkel trail you can follow, with helpful signs identifying what you see. Trunk Bay is an excellent place to spot sea turtles and rays. Reefs full of fish are at both ends of the beach. Look for parrot fish, snappers, tang, and trunkfish and for caves and ledges at the western reef. Snorkel trail, picnic area, snack bar, souvenir shop, snorkel rentals. *North shore.*

CINNAMON BAY

At well over half a mile, this is the island's longest beach. It can be windy here and is a good windsurfing spot. **Snorkeling:** It's especially good along the rocky east end. Watersports center with snorkel and windsurfer rentals, snorkeling and scuba diving lessons and excursions, campground, restaurant, store. *North shore.*

MAHO BAY

Beginning swimmers like the exceptionally calm waters and the fact that the water is so shallow for a long way out. **Snorkeling:** It's a good place to spot rays and turtles. *North shore.*

FRANCIS BAY

A long, narrow beach runs along this well-protected bay and the water is very calm. **Snorkeling:** Look for coral at the western edge, sea turtles out in the bay, octopus at the east end. *North shore.*

WATERLEMON BAY/LEINSTER BAY

The beach here is tiny and a bit rocky but Waterlemon Bay, which is at the eastern edge of big and beautiful Leinster Bay, is an outstanding snorkel spot. **Snorkeling:** Watch for sea turtles, stingrays, octopus, peacock flounder, sponges, seastars (starfish), and schools of parrot fish. *North shore.*

129

SALTPOND BAY

You'll find fewer people at this wide beach than at many of the north shore beaches. **Snorkeling:** Look in the rocky areas for octopus and moray eels. This is also a good spot to see angelfish, grunts, snappers, turtles, conch, and stingrays. *South shore.*

LITTLE LAMESHUR BAY

Expect to find few people at this out-of-the-way beach. **Snorkeling:** You'll see all kinds of fish among the eastern rocks and along the western shoreline. This is also a good spot for sea turtles and rays. *South shore.*

SNORKELING HINTS

❑When it is sunny, you'll see more and it will be clearer if you snorkel between 8 a.m. to 10 a.m.

❑Protect the reefs. Coral is extremely fragile and it grows very slowly. Never touch it, never step on it with your flippers, and never anchor your boat in coral.

❑Watch out for black blobs with spikes that nestle among the rocks. These are sea urchins and they sting. The bigger they are, the worse the pain.

❑Parrot fish cover themselves with sleeping bags at night. If you spot some things that look like little plastic sacs, it could be sleeping parrot fish. They make their own little sleeping bags each night.

❑Speaking of parrot fish, they are big beach builders. They and other reef fish eat algae that grows on coral and inadvertently also take in bits of the coral skeletons, which they later excrete as sand!

❑If you want to dive a bit deeper than you can comfortably snorkel, but don't want tanks on your back, try **Snuba**. The air tank remains on a float above the water and follows you around. *Reservations necessary. Mon.-Sat. 11 a.m. and 1 p.m., Sun. 1 p.m. $49. 340-693-8063. Trunk Bay.*

DIVING

DIVING

The underwater geography around St. John is shallow but there are still great 30' to 50' dives. **Cruz Bay Watersports** takes certified divers out every morning for a two-tank dive. Pick up is 8:15 a.m. at the Westin Dock and 8:45 a.m. at the National Park Dock. You're in the water a few minutes later. The daily afternoon trip (1:15 p.m. at the Westin Dock and 1:45 p.m. at the National Park Dock) is a one-tank dive but they also take snorkelers and give scuba lessons. *Morning $75; afternoon $55. 340-776-6234. Cruz Bay.*

BOATING

DAY SAILS

You'll find a number of charter boats in Cruz Bay that will take you out for a half- or full-day sail or even a sunset sail. **Hurricane Alley** features a 51' Hinkley, which takes a maximum of six people, and a stunning 67' schooner, Starlight, which takes a maximum of 14 people. A full-day sail on either vessel includes a long sail, a buffet lunch at anchor, and an afternoon snorkel. Starlight also heads out on Sunset Cruises, which include an hour-and-a-half sail with wine, beer, rum punch, and hors d'oeuvres and on Fridays Starlight sails over to Foxy's and White Bay on Jost Van Dyke in the British Virgin Islands. Hurricane Alley also offers a half-day snorkel trip on a powerboat which stops at two snorkel spots on other islands. *Per person rates: Full day on Hinkley $100, on Starlight $80; sunset cruise $50; BVI cruise $90 plus fee for customs; powerboat snorkel trip $40. 340-776-6256. Mongoose Junction.*

RENTING POWERBOATS

When the water is calm, it can be a wonderful adventure to rent your own little powerboat and head out to an uninhabited island for the day. You can easily go to Grass, Mingo, or Lovango Cay, where there are little beaches, or to Whistling Cay, where there is the ruin of a house along a beach. You can even go to the British Virgin Islands (see page 97). **Ocean Runner Powerboat Rentals** rents 20', 22', 25', and 27' powerboats, each with a bimini, VHS radio, and cooler. You can hire a captain if you want, and rent snorkel and fishing gear. *$195-$315 per day. 340-693-8809. Wharfside Village, Cruz Bay.*

SEA KAYAKING

Rent a kayak or go on a guided excursion with **Arawak Expeditions**. Three-hour trips leave at 9 a.m. and 2 p.m. for a nearby cay and some snorkeling. Full-day trips depart at 10 a.m. for several uninhabited cays and snorkeling. They also have overnight and multi-day camping trips. *$50 half-day, $80 full-day. 340-693-8312.*

131

THE BEST OF ST. THOMAS AND ST. JOHN A-Z

The best **ARMAGNACS** at Hotel 1829...the best **BEACH** would be Magen's Bay or Trunk Bay...the best **CONCH FRITTERS** are at Sandra's Terrace...some bests for **DAY TRIPS**, Tortola and Jost...the best for **ELEGANCE**, The Ritz-Carlton...the best **FAMILY** Resort, The Westin...some of the best **GARMENTS** at Nicole Miller...for the best **HIDEAWAY**, Caneel Bay...and the best **INNKEEPERS** are the Borns...for great **JAZZ**, it's La Tapa...the best **KAYAKING** is at West Indies Windsurfing, and the very best **LICORICE** at A Chew or Two, of course...and the best **MARGARITAS** at La Tapa...for great **NAUTICAL GIFTS**, it's Shipwreckers...the greatest **OUT ISLAND**, Water, of course... and the best **PARASAILING** is at the east end of St. Thomas...the best **QUESADILLAS** at J.J.'s... the best **ROMANTIC LUNCH** has to be Virgilio's...and **ROMANTIC DINNER**, Chateau Bordeaux...the best **SPEEDBOAT**, Rush Hour...and the best **TENNIS** at Caneel Bay...the easiest **UNDERWATER** experience is Snuba...the best **VIEWS** are everywhere ...and the best **WINE CELLARS** can be found at Virgilio's and Epernay and Room With A View...the best **XERES** cocktail at Tickles ...and maybe the best frozen **YOGURT** at Haagen Dazs in Red Hook...and, the best **ZUPPA DI CIPOLLE** at Romano's.

SECTION III

WATER ISLAND
&
HASSEL ISLAND

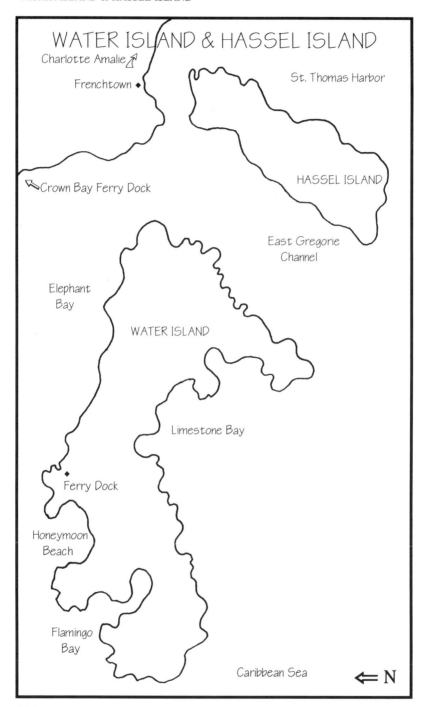

WATER ISLAND & HASSEL ISLAND

Charlotte Amalie

Frenchtown ◆

St. Thomas Harbor

Crown Bay Ferry Dock

HASSEL ISLAND

East Gregorie Channel

Elephant Bay

WATER ISLAND

Limestone Bay

◆ Ferry Dock

Honeymoon Beach

Flamingo Bay

Caribbean Sea

⇐ N

WATER ISLAND

Less than a half-mile off the south shore of St. Thomas lies Water Island, a hilly two-mile-long island. It happens to be the fourth largest U.S. Virgin Island but what many people still don't know is that Water Island officially became the fourth Virgin Island on December 12, 1996.

Like its sister Virgin Islands, Water Island is quite hilly and has a curvaceous shoreline. It's also quite small at just under 492 acres. The island is about two miles long and its width varies from about one-third of a mile to about 400 yards. The highest point is 294'. It has a pretty little curve of a beach known as Honeymoon Beach and another beach quite good for snorkeling. There's also one very casual and very modest, small hotel. There are private residences, and an occasional car, but there is not one single restaurant or store on the island.

A DAYTIME BEACH ADVENTURE

For a great daytime beach adventure, head over to Crown Bay Marina, which is just west of Charlotte Amalie and catch the ferry to Water Island. It runs quite often and it's easy to go for a full day or just the morning or afternoon. (*See page 137 for the complete schedule*). The fare is $3 per person each way.

You'll see the little boat alongside the dock in front of Tickles Restaurant and Bar at Crown Bay Marina. It's a neat, open-air affair. Just hop on and wait. The pilot will show up soon enough (he's usually off getting supplies for the island). The trip over to Water Island takes five minutes. There are absolutely no facilities here so you'll need to bring everything you might want to have with you—towels, sun screen, a cooler with water and sodas, and perhaps lunch. Or have lunch at Tickles before you go or on your return.

There's a good swimming beach and a good snorkeling beach. Honeymoon Beach is a gentle curve of white sand and the water is very calm here. It's over a little rise but you can walk to it from the ferry dock. Just follow the road. This is a great beach for sunning and relaxing. On the other side of the island is a coral beach, called Limestone Beach, that is rocky on the feet but does have good snorkeling. This beach is a bit of a haul (a very long hike up and down) but you can sometimes find a ride. You can also hike to see the remnants of an old fort up on the hill. It's recently been painted but still is not much to look at. However, the views are terrific. Ask someone at the dock for directions. If you plan to hike around, do bring plenty of water.

GETTING AWAY FROM IT ALL
FOR A DAY, OR A WEEK, OR EVEN TWO

If you really want to get away from everything and can be content with comfortable but basic furnishings, you might want to stay on Water Island at the Limestone Reef Terraces. It's on a hilltop and the views of St. Thomas are superb during the day and magical at night. This is a very modest place. There is a little group of ten motel-like efficiencies. Each one is very simply furnished but has a kitchenette and a small sleeping/living area. Ceiling fans and louvered windows open to the breezes keep it cool. Outside, you have your own dining table and chairs on a large, communal terrace. You'll discover that it is delightful to dine outside day and night. The terrace is also a pleasant place for sunning and for evening cocktails. There is no pool here but the beach is just a walk down the hill and management will drive you there or anywhere else on the island that you wish to go.

This is the place to come when you really want to get away from everything, and can be content with very plain accommodations. The pleasures here are of the simple kind. There's not much to do except sit around and think or read and look at the views. Or take a walk or head down to Honeymoon Beach for a peaceful swim or over to Limestone Beach for a good snorkel. Since there are no restaurants here, you will need to do your own cooking, and since there are no stores here, you will need to bring supplies from St. Thomas. It can be quite an adventure to occasionally take the ferry to town for supplies or just to wander around.

By the way, you're not completely isolated if you are staying here, since you can take the ferry back to the marina and have breakfast, lunch, or dinner at Tickles Restaurant and Bar. One day a week the ferry goes on to Charlotte Amalie and three nights a week you can also go to town in the evening. Tuesday, Friday, and Saturday the ferry will drop you anywhere you want along the waterfront in Charlotte Amalie. Just be sure to get back to the marina by 10 p.m. or you'll miss the last trip back to Water Island and you'll be stranded on St. Thomas. For $20 for one to four people (more for returns after 10:30 p.m.), you can also charter the ferry to downtown whenever you want.

10 units. Also a three-bedroom house for rent up on a hill with beautiful views and a car. For reservations: Island Vacations, 10 Cleveland Ln., R.D. 4, Princeton, N.J. 08540. Res: 800-872-USA-USVI or 732-329-6309; Fax: 732-329-6919. Local tel: 340-774-2148. http.//www.nerc.com/ ~ vacation. $80-$95 per night for two people, which includes maid service, free transportation around Water Island, use of snorkel equipment.

St. Thomas-Water Island Ferry Schedule

Monday-Saturday

From St. Thomas	From Water Island
6:45 a.m.	7:00 a.m.
7:15 a.m.	7:30 a.m.
8:00 a.m.	8:15 a.m.
11:00 a.m.	11:15 a.m.
12:00 p.m.	12:15 p.m.
2:00 p.m.	2:15 p.m.
4:00 p.m.	4:15 p.m.
5:00 p.m.	5:15 p.m.
6:00 p.m.	6:15 p.m.

NIGHT RUNS (Tues., Fri., Sat.)

9:00 p.m.	9:15 p.m.
10:00 p.m.	(with advance notice)

Sunday

8:00 a.m.	8:15 a.m.
12:00 p.m.	12:15 p.m.
5:00 p.m.	5:15 p.m.

HASSEL ISLAND

It can be a bit of a hassle getting to Hassel Island but if you are the adventurous type, you might find it a lot of fun.

This is the island that sits right in the middle of St. Thomas harbor. Although there are a few private residences, most of the 135-acre island is part of the Virgin Islands National Park. Trails have not been maintained but if you want a bit of a rugged hike, it is possible to follow them. The National Register of Historic Places lists four spots on this island, including an old coal mining station and shipyard. These are unrestored and pretty much in ruin at the moment. Occasionally there are guided hikes. *Call 340-775-6238 or 340-776-6201, ext. 252 for information.*

So how do you get here? Try **Launch with Larry** (*340-690-80730*), which is the Water Island ferry, or check with "The Reefer" ferry that runs between downtown Charlotte Amalie and Marriott Frenchman's Reef Hotel. Sometimes they will drop you off and pick you up.

PRACTICAL INFORMATION

Banking

On St. Thomas, Citibank has a branch at Havensight and Chase Manhattan has four branches, including one on the Waterfront in Charlotte Amalie. Chase Manhattan also has a branch in Cruz Bay on St. John. ATM machines are often on the blink, so please don't count on getting cash from them.

Crime

On St. Thomas, act carefully, the same way you would in any city. Watch for pickpockets in Charlotte Amalie. Don't walk at night; instead, drive or take cabs. On St. John, it is safe to walk around Cruz Bay at night. Don't leave valuables visible in your car, even if it is locked, and don't leave your wallet in your hotel room.

Currency and Credit Cards

The currency is the U.S. dollar.

Car Rentals

If you are staying at a resort, you will probably find it easier to get there first and then rent a car. Virtually all car rental agencies will pick you up and some resorts have rental agencies right on the premises. Cars run about $50 a day. Avis, Budget, and Hertz are at the St. Thomas airport and other St. Thomas locations and Avis and Hertz are on St. John. On-season, it is best to make your reservations well ahead of time to be sure of getting a car.

Customs

Each U.S. visitor, including children, can return with (or mail) $1,200 worth of duty-free imported goods from the U.S. Virgin Islands every 30 days. U.S. residents 21 years of age or over may return with 4 litres of liquor duty-free (5 litres if one is locally produced, like Virgin Islands rum). You clear customs either in St. Thomas or if you are flying via San Juan, sometimes San Juan.

Documents

You can get by with an expired passport (not more than 5 years) or a birth certificate with a raised seal plus a photo I.D., but if you have a current passport, bring it. It makes getting back home easier and once you see how close the British Virgin Islands are, you'll probably want to head there for a day and you MUST have a valid passport to enter the BVI.

Driving

First of all, it's on the left. Secondly, these are extremely hilly islands and the roads are steep and curvy. Be very careful when it rains. Islanders drive fast and tailgate. Try to ignore the tailgating or pull over and let them pass. Main roads are well-paved but side roads aren't. This is particularly true on St. John.

Getting to and from St. Thomas and St. John
You can fly to St. Thomas's Cyril E. King airport from many U.S. cities on American, Delta, and U.S. Airways. American also flies direct from many U.S. cities to Puerto Rico, and connects with American Eagle flights to St. Thomas. In addition, there are numerous charter companies that fly to St. Thomas. St. John has no airport, but ferries run regularly from both Charlotte Amalie and Red Hook on St. Thomas (*see ferry schedule, page 140*).

Public Holidays
The USVI celebrate all major U.S. holidays. Banks and virtually all shops will be closed on these days. Carnival is a two week festival. On St. Thomas, it is tied into Easter. On St. John it ends on the Fourth of July.

Taxis and Buses
For taxi information, see pages 44-45. Votran buses also cover popular routes on both St. Thomas and St. John.

Telephone
The area code for the USVI is 340. When you are in the USVI, use the seven-digit number, even if you are calling from one U.S. Virgin Island to another.

Time
It's Atlantic Standard Time, which is one hour ahead of Eastern Standard Time. However, the USVI does not switch to Daylight Savings Time and during these months they are on the same time as the U.S. eastern time zone.

Weather
People often think that the further south one goes, the hotter it gets. Not true! The USVI temperatures hover around 75 degrees in the winter, 85 degrees in the summer and the trade winds almost always blow. New York City can be much hotter in August than the USVI!

What to Bring
Sunscreen (the USVI are only 18 degrees from the equator and the sun is strong all year long), bug repellant, casual clothes. In the evening at the nicer restaurants on St. Thomas, casual elegant resortwear is appropriate, including long pants and collared shirts for men. St. John is more relaxed, although the the two large resorts have restaurant dress codes. Bring sturdy shoes if you want to hike and perhaps a light sweater as evenings can be cool.

FERRY SCHEDULES

BETWEEN CHARLOTTE AMALIE, ST. THOMAS AND CRUZ BAY, ST. JOHN

The Charlotte Amalie ferry dock for this ferry is right at Waterfront Highway, across the road and a bit west of Hibiscus Alley. The ferry ride takes about 45 minutes and the one-way fare is $7. Going to St. John they collect the money on the boat, but from St. John you need to buy a ticket at the booth. Call Transportation Services (*340-776-6282*).

From Charlotte Amalie	From Cruz Bay
9:00 a.m.	7:15 a.m.
11:00 a.m.	9:15 a.m.
1:00 p.m.	11:15 p.m.
3:00 p.m.	1:15 p.m.
4:00 p.m.	2:15 p.m.
5:30 p.m.	3:45 p.m.

BETWEEN RED HOOK, ST. THOMAS AND CRUZ BAY, ST. JOHN

The ferry ride takes about 15 to 20 minutes and the one-way fare is $3 for adults, $1 for children under 12. There is a ticket booth at both docks. Call Transportation Services for additional information (*340-776-6282*).

From Red Hook	From Cruz Bay
6:30 a.m.	on the hour
7:30 a.m	6 a.m.-11 p.m
on the hour 8 a.m.-midnight	

BETWEEN CHARLOTTE AMALIE AND MARRIOTT FRENCHMAN'S REEF

A cute little ferry runs between the resort and town, and you can take it from town to the resort to dine or swim at Morningstar Beach. The one-way fare is $4 and it leaves from Waterfront Highway, right across from Rolex.

From Charlotte Amalie
Mon.-Sat. every hour on the hour, 9:00 a.m.-5:00 p.m.
Sun. every hour on the half hour, 9:30 a.m.-4:30 p.m.

From Marriott Frenchman's Reef
Mon.-Sat. every hour on the half hour, 8:30 a.m.-4:30 p.m.
Sun. every hour on the hour, 9:00 a.m.-4:00 p.m.

INDEX

142

ABOUT THE AUTHOR

Pamela Acheson was Vice-President and Director of Marketing for a Fortune-500 publishing company in New York City until she and her husband headed south over a decade ago. Since their successful escape she has lived in, explored, and written extensively about Florida and the Caribbean.

The Best of St. Thomas and St. John, U.S. Virgin Islands is the latest in the "Best" series, which includes *The Best of the British Virgin Islands,* the award-winning *The Best Romantic Escapes in Florida,* and with her husband Richard Myers, *More of the Best Romantic Escapes in Florida.*

In addition to her own books and consulting, Ms. Acheson regularly contributes to many guidebooks including *Fodor's Caribbean, Fodor's Virgin Islands, Fodor's Florida, Fodor's Walt Disney World,* and *Fodor's Cruises and Ports of Call.*

Her articles and photographs have appeared in numerous publications including *Travel and Leisure, Caribbean Travel and Life,* and *Florida Travel and Life.* She lives and travels in Florida and the Virgin Islands with her husband.